MORE
than the
SCORE

ALSO BY MATT FULKS

NONFICTION

The Sportscaster's Dozen: Off the Air with Southeastern Legends, 1998

Behind the Stats: Tennessee's Coaching Legends, 1996

COLLABORATIONS

Tales from the Royals Dugout with Denny Matthews (Updated), 2006

Tales from the Royals Dugout with Denny Matthews, 2004

Good as Gold: Techniques for Fundamental Baseball with Frank White, 2004

The Road to Canton with Marcus Allen, 2003

Tales from the Oakland Raiders with Tom Flores, 2003

*Play by Play: 25 Years of Royals on Radio
with Denny Matthews and Fred White, 1999*

EDITED

Echoes of Kansas Basketball, 2006

CBS Sports Presents: Stories from the Final Four, 2000

*Super Bowl Sunday:
The Day America Stops, Presented by CBS Sports, 2000*

MORE
than the
SCORE

Kansas City Sports Memories

Celebrating 10 years of Metro Sports

Matt Fulks

Requests for permission to make copies of any part of the work should be mailed to:
    Communications Manager
    Metro Sports/Time Warner Cable
    6550 Winchester, Kansas City, Missouri 64133

Published by Metro Sports Books
Coordinated by Angie Paprocki
Edited by Carol Rothwell
Interior Designed by Derek Kilgore and Karla Eddy
Cover Designed by Derek Kilgore
Cover Photo and Back Cover Photos by Gregg Riess
Book Printed by Service Printing & Graphics, Inc., Kansas City, Missouri
Pictures courtesy of Metro Sports, Gregg Riess, Jim Chappell, Kansas City Royals, Kansas City Wizards, Kansas City Chiefs, Negro League Museum, San Diego Charges, University of Missouri, Kansas State University, Rockhurst High School, AP Graphics, AP Photo and Rich Clarkson/NCAA Photos, Dave Stewart, Phil Dixon, Steve Beaumont and Rich Brown.

ATTENTION: SCHOOLS AND BUSINESSES Metro Sports books are available at quantity discounts with bulk purchase for education, business, or sales promotional use. For information, please write to: Communications Manager, Metro Sports, 6550 Winchester, Kansas City, Missouri 64133

All profits from the sale of the book are going to the Metro Sports High School Athletic Scholarship Fund.

More than the Score: Kansas City Sports Memories/Celebrating 10 years of Metro Sports; Matt Fulks.

ISBN – 10: 0-9791473-0-1
ISBN – 13: 978-0-9791473-0-2

Printed in the United States of America

To my mom, Sharon Fulks.
Besides the obvious reason of, you know, life,
this book isn't possible
without your constant love and support,
plus the additional baby-sitting hours.

~

To my uncle, Gary Fulks,
who lost a battle with cancer the day
I signed the contract to write this book.
It's through your counsel, support and nudging
I went into broadcasting and, eventually, writing.

~

And, a special dedication to the athletes and coaches
who have given Kansas City such a rich sports history;
To the sportswriters, broadcasters and fans
who have helped mold those memories;
To everyone at Metro Sports
for keeping those moments alive for the past decade.

Table of Contents

Acknowledgments

It seems like I'm always getting myself into these messes — trying to write a book in six weeks or less. Truth told, if it weren't for some incredible people, I'd still be hunkered over the computer with blood-shot eyes, debating between which was the biggest bust, Juan Gonzalez, Bam Morris or Morganna "The Kissing Bandit." Although it seemingly would take me a decade just to thank everyone who played a part in what you're about to read, I need to personally thank the following:

To Karla Eddy for a great job of designing this under a tight deadline. To Gregg Riess, who took some wonderful photographs, particularly the book's cover. To Metro Sports' Derek Kilgore, who turned Gregg's photo into a cool cover.

To John Denison and John Sprugel at Metro Sports for coming up with the idea for this book and then trusting me to pull it off. Through brainstorming sessions and bribery, several people helped come up with the voting lists that were whittled down to top-10 lists, including — Erik Ashel, Chris Gough, Leif Lisec, Curtis Lorenz, Brad Porter, Mick Shaffer, Herbie Teope and Dave Stewart, who also came up with a typically humorous "High Five" for Chapter 20.

Also at Metro Sports, Carol Rothwell, who did a wonderful job of editing this book. Transforming that rough draft into something readable took a keen eye and incredible patience. When it comes to Metro, though, the biggest thanks goes to Angie Paprocki, who did more for this project than anyone else, present company included.

To Neil Harwell, one of my mentors and, let's face it, the reason Metro Sports and I hooked up in the first place. Your anecdotes, proofreading and friendship were vital to this book.

To the librarians and research assistants at the various branches of the Johnson County Library and the Plaza branch of the Kansas City Public Library.

To Jim Chappell for giving us full access to your restaurant, which is one of the best pieces of sports history in Kansas City, even if it is only 20 years old. To Deron Cherry, Len Dawson, Scott Wedman, Frank White and Fred White, five of Kansas City's "legends" who offered personal memories for the "High Five" lists. To Denny Matthews for going back 30 years and providing the list of the top-10 Scouts and some stories that didn't make the book. To Sid Bordman for your wonderful anecdotes and top-10 lists for the Blues and A's. To Steve Beaumont, Rich Brown, Pete Campbell and Brad Doolittle for offering your personal memories that are used throughout the book.

To former Chiefs lineman Pellom McDaniels, who's one of life's great success stories, for helping edit and navigate the chapter on the "Birth of the Negro Leagues." We look forward to having you back in Kansas City. To Bob Kendrick, who took time out of his schedule during one of the roughest times of his life, to assist with the chapters on the Negro Leagues and Buck O'Neil. Buck, indeed, wore off on you. To Mark Stallard, a great writer, for helping me keep my sanity a couple times and being a good sounding board for the KU chapters.

To Dave and Kathy Minich for giving me a hideaway in the middle of Missouri a few times so I could work on this project.

To the group of friends and family who serve as my core support and guidance, I owe a mountain of gratitude: Steve Treece, who offered top-10 list ideas (even if they were all Mizzou related) during our Saturday morning rides; Chris Garrett, who took the first tour of Chappell's with me; Jim Wissel; Chris and Melissa Hartwick; Bill and Brandy Nolan; Dennis and Caroline Odell; Mike and Liz Straughn; Paul and Jane Talley; plus Tim and Amy Brown, who were a source of endless encouragement and stress relief during the entire project. Your friendship is appreciated more than I'll ever show. I have to say that I prayed a lot during this project, particularly the last couple weeks. They were like the last six miles of a marathon and the last 20 miles of a century. So, without Christ this isn't possible. A final special thanks to my favorite in-laws, Todd and Pat Burwell; my parents, Fred and Sharon; along with my best friend, Libby, who kept her sanity when I lost mine; and our three children, Helen, Charlie and Aaron, who were subjected to more "Blue's Clues" and "Mickey Mouse Clubhouse" episodes than any one child should be in a lifetime, but they love me anyway.

Thank you, all.

Introduction

Inevitably, the question comes up when I'm talking with someone who knows me.

"So, what are you working on these days?"

About six weeks ago, my answer was simply, "I'm writing a book on the history of Kansas City sports."

Then, dead silence, usually accompanied by a look akin to the person who learns that one of his best friends has two uvulas. Then, laughter, usually accompanied by the heckling that the person gives his best friend with the two uvulas.

The reaction of shock and bewilderment was easy to understand. After all, Kansas City has a long and unique sports history, dating back to the 1800s, when professional baseball came to town in the form of the Antelopes. They were an independent team that played in 1866, coincidentally 10 years before the National League was formed.

The coincidence? That number. Ten. Usually, it's considered the number of Olympic perfection and Bo Derek. In Kansas City, it's also Dick Howser. Trent Green. Half of Frank White's 20. Double George Brett's 5. The Chiefs won Super Bowl IV during their 10th season of existence. And, in December 2006, 10 marked the number of years Metro Sports has been on the air.

The idea for this book started in the fall of 2005 … more than, well, 10 months ago. At the time, the concept — celebrating Metro Sports' 10th birthday with a collection of top-10 lists that highlight Kansas City's sports history — seemed both unique and challenging. When we agreed in September 2006 to write the book, it indeed, turned out to be both enlightening and stressful. After all, we're talking about more than 100 (10 x 10, by the way) years of hall-of-fame athletes, championship teams, inspirational moments, along with some of the biggest characters and duds in sports history.

About that same time, a good friend of mine and Metro Sports' first general manager, Neil Harwell, started teaching a class at our church based on the *New York Times* bestseller, *The Traveler's Gift* by Andy Andrews. In that book, the main character travels through time and learns valuable life lessons from significant people in world history. Nearly every week of the eight-week study, Harwell stressed that "authors don't know everything."

I laughed every time he said it because, as I've learned during each of the first 10 books I've written so far, that's incredibly true. I know very little and have trouble remembering what I do know. Harwell's statement also made me laugh because it certainly fit along the lines of *More Than the Score*. Although I've lived in the Kansas City area most of my life, setting out alone to write a book on the most memorable moments in Kansas City's sports history — let alone trying to do it in less than two months — is insane. The vain thought that I could be that person to pull it off is crazier.

Thankfully, during one of our planning meetings, someone suggested we let the fans choose through online voting. And, you did.

A group of people from Metro Sports sat down on two occasions and came up with ideas for nearly 20 lists and the events or people to fill those lists. Then, for more than a month, you as fans had a chance to vote for your favorites and add some of your own. The next 200 pages or so are the results of your voting and my writing. (Talk about print-on-demand.)

What you are about to read is a snapshot of the most memorable moments and people throughout Kansas City's sports history based on your selections. It's not an encyclopedia of sports for this area. It's simply a highlight of the most memorable moments, athletes and coaches in our city's history.

As with any book of lists and rankings, seemingly key events might be left out. For instance, the construction of the Kansas Speedway and NASCAR's subsequent presence in Kansas City were on a couple lists, but received very few votes. Although those are important marks in our city's sports history, you've just read all you're going to read about them in this book. Same with UMKC. The 'Roos had a couple moments, but received a minimal amount of votes. Some might argue that's based solely on popularity; others might say it's a matter of the rich history of Kansas City's sports.

One thing you will see scattered throughout the book is something called "A Legend's High Five." We thought it would be interesting to talk with a few of the notable athletes and broadcasters from Kansas City to find out their personal top-five moments. So, there are lists from three athletes who were stars with their respective teams — Deron Cherry (Chiefs), Scott Wedman (Kings) and Frank White (Royals).

And, four broadcasters offered their top memories — Len Dawson (yes, the former Chiefs QB, who's known as much these days for his TV and radio work), Neil Harwell, Dave Stewart and Fred White.

What you are about to read is the first book of its kind in Kansas City.

It encompasses everything from the birth of the Negro National League, to the Chiefs and Royals championship seasons, to the top athletes and coaches at the "local" Big 12 schools — Kansas, Kansas State, Missouri, to some of the most inspirational events we've experienced.

My hope is that as you read this, you'll gain a better understanding of our city's sports history, or at least have something to debate with your buddies when you're out watching a game. It did both of those things for me. And, it made me a little smarter, at least when someone would ask me what I was working on.

"I'm writing a book on Kansas City's most memorable sports moments."

The heckling stopped. "That sounds interesting."

Maybe so. You be the judge.

Matt Fulks
November 9, 2006

◆◆◆◆◆◆◆◆◆◆ Section I ◆◆◆◆◆◆◆◆◆

BEST and WORST OVERALL

Chapter 1

The Top Moment:
Royals Win 1985 World Series

*There are two truths when it comes to the 1985
World Series: Royals fans won't forget it, and
seemingly all other baseball fans in the country,
particularly those on the east side of Missouri,
refuse to remember it.*

The passion the 1985 World Series holds with fans in Kansas and Missouri partially helps explain why it was the fans' overwhelming pick for this book as the Greatest Moment in Kansas City Sports History.

The memories might also come from the way that team won. They never gave up. Whether it was during a losing streak in September or facing elimination against Toronto and St. Louis, down 3-games-to-1 in both the American League Championship Series and the World Series, the Royals felt confident that they could win. At times they were more like the puppy with a Doberman's mentality.

The old adage in life — sometimes it's better to be lucky than good — certainly applied to the '85 Royals. Sure, they were good, winning 91 games. But a little luck went a long way throughout the season, particularly in the postseason.

"We might not have had the best talent in 1985, but we were the best *team* in 1985," says then-general manager John Schuerholz.

Indeed. There was a point when the 1985 Royals didn't even look as if they were the best team in the American League West, let alone in all of baseball.

At mid-July's All-Star break, the Royals barely held their heads above the .500 mark, at 44-42. They trailed the AL West-leading California Angels by 7½

Courtesy of the Kansas City Royals

Heroes Welcome

games. A tell-tale sign of the way the Royals played in the first half of 1985 is that they had only one player, George Brett, representing them at the All-Star Game. (Manager Dick Howser was a coach for the AL that year.) It was the first time since 1977 that the Royals, who had five players on the AL squad just three years earlier, had only one representative.

Six days after the All-Star Game, still 7½ games back, the Royals woke up and went on a seven-game winning streak, and won nine-out-of-10 games. They went 25-15 in their first 40 contests after the All-Star break.

During the month of July, a second-year pitcher named Bret Saberhagen emerged as a potential star of the pitching staff. Saberhagen went 5-1 with a 2.05 earned run average and was selected as the AL Pitcher of the Month.

And, of course, there was Brett, who was the AL Player of the Month in July with a .432 batting average, .726 slugging percentage, seven home runs and 24 runs batted in.

With the Angels in sight, the Royals remained hot throughout much of the final two months, including an eight-game winning streak in early September. Much like they did with their post-All-Star-break streak, after September's eight-game winning streak ended the Royals didn't slow down. They won 12-of-13 in that stretch.

Their only hiccup came in the middle of September. At that time, Seattle swept the Royals in a four-game series at Royals Stadium. Ten days later, the Twins swept the Royals in Minnesota. Fortunately, the Angels fared just as poorly.

Finally, after taking three-of-four from the Angels in Kansas City in early October, the Royals clinched the Western Division title at home with a 5-4 win over Oakland on October 5, the next-to-the-last day of the regular season. Albeit by one game, it was the latest they had ever clinched the division. But, for the second time in as many years, the Royals were headed to the postseason.

Still, the Royals' 91-71 record was anything but stellar when it came to the four teams that made up baseball's playoffs in 1985. In fact, it was the worst. The Royals' opponent from the AL East, Toronto, carried a 99-62 mark. On the other side, the Los Angeles Dodgers went in at 95-67, with Whitey Herzog's St. Louis club boasting a 101-61 record.

KANSAS CITY'S
10 MOST MEMORABLE SPORTS MOMENTS

- ⑩ KU wins NCAA Tournament at Kemper
- ⑨ A's bring Major League Baseball to KC
- ⑧ Chiefs move to Kansas City
- ⑦ George Brett's homer sends Royals to World Series
- ⑥ Death of Derrick Thomas
- ⑤ Birth of the Royals
- ④ Birth of the Negro Leagues
- ③ Life of Buck O'Neil
- ② Chiefs win Super Bowl IV
- ① Royals win 1985 World Series

The can-do, never-say-die attitude, however, that served the Royals so well during the 1985 regular season carried over into the playoffs and the World Series, led by what's best described as a total team effort and a manager who believed in his players.

◆ ◆ ◆

Certainly a lot could be said for the postseason play in '85 of one of the club's marquee players: George Brett.

Brett accomplished a feat that's nearly impossible in baseball — single-handedly leading the Royals to a win in Game 3 of the American League Championship Series against Toronto. In baseball, with nine players on the field and a batter getting only four to five chances a game, it's impractical to think that a player other than the pitcher can take over a game. But, Brett did just that. After the Royals dropped the first two games at home, the chances of advancing looked bleak. In the third game, Brett went four-for-four with two homers and a double, and he scored four of the club's six runs. Defensively, he made one of the best plays of his career when he backhanded a grounder by Lloyd Moseby and threw out Damaso Garcia at home plate.

As Joe McGuff wrote in *The Kansas City Star* on October 12: "If you were there, you saw a performance that will become a part of baseball's post-season lore along with Don Larsen's perfect World Series game, Babe Ruth's called-shot home run and Reggie Jackson's three home runs in the sixth game of the 1977 Series."

Although the Royals lost the next game and had to battle back from a 3-games-to-1 deficit against Toronto, things might've worked out differently had they not won Game 3 behind Brett.

Brett, incidentally, didn't let up during the World Series, batting .370 with 10 hits and five runs against the Cardinals.

◆ ◆ ◆

Of course, anytime the 1985 World Series is discussed and debated, there's ultimately a mention of "the call" at first base in Game 6. Assuming you haven't lived in a hole for the past 20 years, you've seen "the call." You've heard about "the call." You've seen and heard about it enough that you could reenact "the call" with your buddies.

However, in case you somehow forgot it, here's how it played out: in the bottom of the ninth inning and the Royals trailing the game 1-0 and the World Series 3 games to 2, pinch-hitter Jorge Orta led off the inning by grounding a ball toward first base. Cardinal first baseman Jack Clark fielded it cleanly and flipped to pitcher Todd Worrell covering first. Although Worrell seemed to touch first before Orta on the bang-bang play, umpire Don Denkinger didn't hesitate in calling Orta safe.

A few batters later, the Royals scored two runs on Dane Iorg's only hit in the Series and won the game, sending the Series to a seventh game. The hit should've turned Iorg into a hero. Instead, with the controversy from earlier that inning, Iorg's hit often remains forgotten in World Series lore.

Even though the Cardinals self-destructed after that play at first and seemingly failed to show up for Game 7, it's that one call that St. Louis fans bring up during any discussion of the "I-70 Series." There's one thing to remember, though.

"We scored the winning run with one out," says pitcher Mark Gubicza. "We still had an out (left in the inning) if the play went differently at first. The way things had been going for us that season, who's to say that whoever was coming up next doesn't hit a home run and we win anyhow? It was a magical season for us.

"(The Cardinals) had every opportunity in the world to come back in Game 7, but we blew them away. ... Hey, they had us down 3 games to 1. If you can't close it out at 3 games to 1, don't blame it on the umpire. Yeah, (the call) went our way ... (But) you have to be able to close out a team when you have them down like that."

◆ ◆ ◆

The glue that held everything together that season for the Royals, especially when the Royals appeared to be out of both the ALCS and the World Series, was manager Dick Howser.

"He was so honest with you," said Gubicza, who won 14 games for the Royals in '85. "If you messed around or did something wrong, he was in your face. But he allowed you to play if you were out there and ready, and he knew you were going to give your best. That's what he was all about. If you had a bad game, he'd say that he put you in position to have a bad game; not that you had a bad game. He was a confidence builder."

"He didn't say a lot," said John Wathan. "He just expected you to work hard."

When the Royals went down 3 games to 1 to the Blue Jays and then the Cardinals, Howser didn't change his style and didn't give up.

"There was no panic (in our club), which I think was a direct reflection on Dick and the fact that he was one of those people who deflected all the criticism and nerves onto himself and absorbed it," said Gubicza, who came up with the Royals in 1984 as a 21-year-old. "He'd always tell us, 'Don't worry about it. Piss on it. We'll get this thing done.' That was his famous line and the only speech he gave pretty much religiously whenever he took the time to make a speech. We knew he was backing us."

On the flip side of the impression Howser left on the young players such as Gubicza, there were the veterans on the field, such as Frank White. Known for his usually flawless defensive play at second, White, who was in his ninth major-league season when Howser took over the Royals in August 1981, proved under Howser that he was a good offensive player, also. White finished seven of his 18 big-league seasons with double-digit home runs, including all five under Howser.

Dick Howser

Courtesy of the Kansas City Royals

White was one of the top offensive threats for the Royals against the Cardinals during the World Series. As the first second baseman since Jackie Robinson to bat cleanup in the World Series, White hit one of the club's two home runs and led the Royals with six RBIs and three doubles.

"Dick saw a complete player in me, for which I'll always be grateful," White said. "He was a true professional. He had been with the Yankees, a club that didn't mess much with young guys. So, from my standpoint from day one, in 1981, he knew how to handle veteran players, which is what we needed at that time. Through his faith in us and our desire to win for him, we had a magical season in 1985."

♦ ♦ ♦

Two players in whom Howser showed great confidence were shortstop Buddy Biancalana, who became a folk hero after batting .188 during the regular season, and outfielder Darryl Motley, who was the beginning and the end for the Royals in Game 7.

During the second inning of the finale, after belting a foul ball down the left-field line and missing a two-run home run by a few feet, Motley got nearly the same pitch from St. Louis' John Tudor. Motley didn't miss the second time and put the Royals ahead, 2-0. In essence, that was the game-winning hit in the Royals' 11-0 win.

"I was trying to hit the ball out of the ballpark," Motley says. "My agent told me before the game that if I did something special, I'd remember it the rest of my life. That home run was a special moment for me."

Oddly, that homer, or at least Motley's thoughts of it, started a year earlier. When the Royals lost to the Detroit Tigers in the 1984 playoffs, it was Motley's pop foul to third that ended the Royals' season.

"When we got on the bus, it bothered me that I popped up," said Motley. "I told myself that if I ever got another chance, I wasn't going to miss the pitch. I got that chance in a bigger way."

Darryl Motley

Courtesy of the Kansas City Royals

And he didn't miss.

During the series with the Cardinals, shortstop Biancalana didn't miss much either. He certainly capitalized on his chances, offensively and defensively. A .205 lifetime hitter with six home runs in six major-league seasons, Biancalana entered the elusive "zone" during the 1985 World Series, batting .278 with two RBIs, two runs scored and a .435 on-base percentage.

Courtesy of the Kansas City Royals

Buddy Biancalana

Oddly, shortly before the apex of his career, minutes before the start of Game 1 of the World Series, Biancalana felt an overwhelming angst that he'd never experienced before.

"I'll never forget sitting on my chair in front of my locker prior to the game, about a half-hour before ABC wanted us on the foul line," Biancalana said. "I started thinking, 'Oh my, this is really intense.'"

He figured he could put on his street clothes and go watch the game on television somewhere; or he could grab his glove, walk down the runway and take the field.

Luckily, he chose the latter.

Along the way, he became a folk hero. Late Night czar David Letterman helped see to that. In mid-August of that season, which happened to be the same year Pete Rose was chasing Ty Cobb's career-hits record, Letterman mentioned Rose's chase of Cobb. He added that another player also was chasing Cobb: Biancalana, who was around 50 major-league career hits, compared to 4,000-plus for Rose.

Letterman brought out a hit-counter periodically and told everyone how Rose and Biancalana did the previous day.

"That definitely got me a lot of notoriety at a time where my play wasn't," said Biancalana. "It was a wonderful experience. There's nothing wrong with some publicity, and I certainly got it."

Not being a sure out at the plate, and making solid plays between Frank White and George Brett, helped Biancalana gain notoriety as a player. He went from late-night prop to an important part of the Royals' puzzle.

So was Motley, who batted .364 in the Series.

Then there was the final out of the Series. As Royals center fielder Willie Wilson jogged to the outfield for the ninth inning of the 11-0 shellacking, he made a prediction to Motley. With the game's winner a foregone conclusion, Wilson proudly told Motley that he would be catching the final out, sealing the Royals' victory. Of course

Motley told the fleet-footed Wilson that this would be one time he'd beat Wilson to the ball.

With two outs, St. Louis' Andy Van Slyke drove a ball toward right-center. As Motley foretold Wilson, he charged over, camped under the ball and clasped it tightly in his glove as the celebrating began.

"I got there first, but I could hear Willie coming," Motley said, laughing, "but he was too late. I caught it and I still have the ball."

The following September, the Royals traded Motley to the Atlanta Braves. His major-league career lasted only six seasons, but he played stints in Japan, the Mexican League and the Independent League. He played until 2002, when he was 42.

After the 1985 World Series, Biancalana made an in-studio appearance with Letterman. Unfortunately, four years later, Biancalana's playing career was finished because of back problems.

1985 seems like a lifetime ago. Especially if you're a Royals' fan. But it can seem like yesterday when baseball's biggest stage is your brightest moment as a player.

"That home run was a special moment for me and one that I'll never forget," said Motley. "I always thought about getting to the big leagues but I never dreamed about playing in the World Series during my second year. I'm really glad we were able to give the fans in Kansas City a champion."

1985 Royals rush the field after winning the World Series.

Chapter 2

Kansas City's Best Wins
and
Heartbreaking Losses

There's something to be said for determination and motivation. The Kansas City Chiefs had both, heading into Super Bowl IV against the Minnesota Vikings in January 1970. After all, to a man, the Green Bay Packers had overmatched the Chiefs in Super Bowl I. Although the Chiefs featured a good offense that year, they didn't have the players in place on the defensive side to be the best team in pro football. The Chiefs realized that ahead of time. The Packers confirmed it.

To make sure it didn't happen again, head coach Hank Stram was determined the team's defense wouldn't be its shortcoming. During the next couple of years, the Chiefs added players such as Emmitt Thomas, Jim Kearney and Jim Marsalis to the defensive backfield, along with linebackers Jim Lynch and Willie Lanier.

There was a little extra motivation, though, heading into Super Bowl IV in January 1970. The game marked the end of the American Football League facing the National Football League. The two leagues merged following that season. Since Lamar Hunt had the foresight to start the AFL, it was only fitting that the Chiefs reach this particular game.

"It was poetic justice that we were the first team to play and represent the American Football League in Super Bowl I," Stram wrote in the book *Super Bowl Sunday: The Day America Stops*. "So, it also seemed appropriate that we were the team to win Super IV, the last championship game before the two leagues officially merged. There was a lot of satisfaction in that."

With the help of the defense that had improved dramatically since Super Bowl I, the Chiefs took the long road to that meeting with the Vikings. Long, indeed.

In spite of a respectable 11-3 regular-season record, the third loss of the year came in the final game, at Oakland, 10-6. That meant the Raiders finished 12-1-1, and won the AFL's Western Division. And, in the four-team playoffs, the Chiefs opened on the road at Shea Stadium against the defending world champion New York Jets.

After a couple field goals, the Chiefs led 6-3 heading into the fourth quarter. With the Jets driving, the Chiefs were flagged for pass interference, giving New York first-and-goal at the 1-yard-line. The Jets failed to score on their first two running plays, setting up a crucial third down. With tears running down his face, Chiefs linebacker Willie Lanier pleaded with the defense to make a stop. The group rallied and held the Jets to a field goal.

"When a grown man comes in the huddle and is crying, that's bonding," said safety Jim Kearney. "We had that bond and we had an incredible desire. We played for the love of the game."

With the game tied at 6-6, the Chiefs went on to score the only touchdown of the contest, when Gloster Richardson caught his only pass of the game from Len Dawson and took it in for a 19-yard touchdown play.

The Chiefs' 13-6 win over New York meant a return trip to Oakland-Alameda County Coliseum, where the Chiefs had lost two weeks earlier. Incidentally, remember how the Chiefs lost only three games that season? Two of them came against the Raiders. In fact, since the first Super Bowl season of 1966, the Raiders held a 7-2 advantage in games between the two teams. (Oh, not to mention that the Raiders embarrassed the Chiefs in the previous postseason meeting between the two teams, 41-6 at Oakland, in a 1968 AFL divisional playoff game.)

This AFL Championship game, the final one in the league's 10-year history, however, became the grudge match expected between the two hated rivals.

Remember, the Chiefs realized they needed to beef up their defense after Super Bowl I. Although it didn't help much in the previous nine games against Oakland, that concept paid off this time.

The Chiefs held Oakland quarterbacks Daryle Lamonica and George Blanda to 154 yards on 17-of-45 passing. The QB tandem also threw four interceptions. Amazingly, the Chiefs lost the ball four times on fumbles, including three times on their end of the field in the fourth quarter, yet the defense stepped up and stopped Oakland each time.

In the end, the Chiefs won 17-7 for their third AFL Championship and second trip to the Super Bowl — this time to New Orleans to face the Minnesota Vikings.

"The Big Easy" still was anything but easy for the Chiefs because of something happening off the field. The day before the Oakland game, a league official had told Stram that Len Dawson's name had surfaced in a betting scandal involving Detroit gambler Donald Dawson (no relation). Shortly before the Raiders game, however, the league official, Mark Duncan, called Stram and told him that everything had been resolved. It was. Until the Chiefs arrived in New Orleans.

"When we got off the bus in New Orleans, we heard the same thing again about Lenny and this betting nonsense," Stram said in 2000. "Only this time it was all over the papers. The story was absolutely absurd!"

In hopes of putting it behind them so they could focus on the game, Stram and Dawson decided to hold a press conference to squash the rumors. NFL commissioner Pete Rozelle, whom Stram called a "great friend," suggested that if they held a press conference, they shouldn't talk about the scandal, only the upcoming game with the Vikings.

"(Rozelle) didn't look at us like we had done something wrong," Stram said. "He was mainly concerned about having a good Super Bowl. I was, too, but I didn't agree with his thoughts on Lenny's press conference."

So, the press conference went on as Stram had envisioned, at 11 p.m. The media seemed satisfied with Dawson's comments.

"Of course he handled everything with typical class and style and grace and dignity," Stram said, "and did a fantastic job, as everybody knows."

Stram's biggest concern was his team's reaction — and possible distraction — due to the reports and all of the questions from the media.

"I told (our team at breakfast the morning after the press conference) what we did the night before," said Stram. "Then I asked if anybody had any questions. E.J. Holub, our center, said, 'Yeah, I've got a question Coach. When are we going to eat? ...

That's how distracted they were. It was amazing how they responded to the situation and rallied around Lenny. The whole team just did a fantastic job of not letting the story affect them, which was obvious in the game."

Oh, yeah, the game.

The Vikings, with an outstanding offense and their defensive "Purple People Eaters," were a team of destiny. In 1969, they ranked first in both offense (379 points) and defense (133 points) in the NFL. The only time they allowed more than 14 points in a game came during a 24-23 season-opening loss to the New York Giants. Offensively, they scored more than 50 points three times in 1969.

The Chiefs weren't too shabby, either, with their top-ranked defense and No. 2-ranked offense in the AFL.

"We still had that shadow of the 'Mickey Mouse League' following us around," says wide receiver Frank Pitts, referring to the AFL's nickname. "We were determined to let everybody know we were going to take care of business."

And, the Chiefs did just that. The confidence they felt going into the contest with Minnesota came out during the game's first two possessions.

After Minnesota marched to the Kansas City 39-yard line, the Chiefs defense awoke and stopped the Vikings. The Chiefs, after starting on their own 17, promptly moved the ball into Minnesota territory, thanks largely to a 20-yard pass play from Dawson to Pitts. Four plays later, Jan Stenerud booted a 48-yard field goal, giving the Chiefs an early 3-0 lead.

The field goal remained a Super Bowl record until Denver's Rich Karlis tied it in Super Bowl XXI. (Buffalo's Steve Christie holds the current record at 54 yards.) Stenerud's record-setting field goal also gave the Chiefs a lead that they wouldn't relinquish.

Kansas City scored on three of its next four possessions, including two more Stenerud field goals and a 5-yard touchdown run by Mike Garrett, and took a 16-0 lead into halftime.

"I remember the run but it wasn't a big run," said Garrett. "What I remember most about scoring is thinking about how the city of Kansas City was going to be beside themselves. They loved us and it was great to be a part of a team that represented Kansas City the way it should be."

The day definitely belonged to Kansas City and the Chiefs. Even after Minnesota scored on a touchdown late in the third quarter, the Chiefs answered on their next possession with a 46-yard pass play from Dawson to Otis Taylor. A 7-yard reverse by Pitts on third-and-7 set up the play.

"That 46-yard touchdown catch and run was the biggest single play of my career," Taylor wrote in his autobiography, *The Need to Win*. "The most beautiful thing about that game and that play was that my Mom was there to see it. When I scored that touchdown, I heard her voice in the crowd yelling, 'That's my baby, that's my baby!' ... It brought tears to my eyes then, and it brings tears to them whenever I think about her now, because she was so special to me."

Dawson, the game's MVP, and his Chiefs won the game convincingly, 23-7.

"We went out and proved that we were bigger and better," said Pitts, who caught three passes for 33 yards, and was the second-leading rusher in the game with 37 yards on three carries — all reverses.

The win gave the city of Kansas City its first pro sports championship since the Monarchs won the 1942 Negro World Series.

With the Chiefs winning Super Bowl IV, a year after the New York Jets became the first AFL team to win the championship by beating the Baltimore Colts, the AFL gained the respect that it deserved. And, that victory might have helped out football as a whole.

"(Those wins have) made pro football what it is today," said Chiefs wide receiver Chris Burford, who played for the Chiefs from 1960-67. "I don't think pro football would be what it is without that competition that existed between the two leagues.

Courtesy of AP Graphics

Coach Hank Stram is carried off the field after winning Super Bowl IV.

"I'm just proud of the fact that I was one of the original guys in the AFL, and the league made it. A number of us contributed, in whatever minor ways, to the league's success. To see what it is today, and knowing that if we hadn't done a decent job early on (the NFL) wouldn't be as strong as it is today, is satisfying."

KANSAS CITY'S BIGGEST SPORTS WINS

10. *Chiefs Beat Houston 28-20 in AFC Divisional Playoffs - January 16, 1994*

On the surface, if one looked at only the score and the fact this was only a divisional playoff game, it seems pretty ho-hum. If only. A week after a 27-24 overtime win against Pittsburgh at Arrowhead, the Chiefs needed quarterback Joe Montana's Mo-Joe in the Astrodome against the Oilers.

Trailing 10-7 after three quarters, the Chiefs scored 21 points in the fourth, including two Montana touchdown passes and a victory-sealing 21-yard touchdown run by Marcus Allen, and secured a spot in the organization's first AFC Championship Game. Despite throwing two interceptions, Montana finished with 299 yards and three touchdown passes against the Oilers.

Not to be overlooked, the Chiefs' defense sacked Houston quarterback (and future Chief) Warren Moon nine times. Albert Lewis, Derrick Thomas, Bennie Thompson and Joe Phillips each had two sacks. Neil Smith added the other.

9. *A Great Dane Leads Wizards from Worst to Champions in 2000*

After posting an embarrassing 8-24 record in 1999, good for last in the West, the Wizards got some much-needed help from a short-term scoring threat and the return of one of the best goalkeepers in the short history of Major League Soccer.

Miklos Molnar, a Denmark native, had done about everything in soccer — played in a World Cup, the European Championships, and the 1992 Olympics. He figured he'd play one year of Major League Soccer in the States before retiring. Thankfully, he spent that one season, 2000, in Kansas City. In addition to leading the

Wizards with 12 goals that year, Molnar helped the Wizards advance in the playoffs by scoring two goals in the third semifinal game against Los Angeles. Then, Molnar scored what turned out to be the game-winning goal in the 11th minute of the championship game against Chicago at Washington's RFK Stadium.

Miklos Molnar

"I remember that Chris Klein was running off the right side, and he passed to the middle. I missed the ball the first time, but I kicked it again and somehow it went in," Molnar said. "It didn't look nice, but it rolled over the line. And that's all that counts. I will never forget that goal."

Another hero was goalkeeper Tony Meola, who had blown out his ACL in 1999. After a 2000 regular season that included an MLS record 16 shutouts in 31 games, Meola won the MLS Cup MVP award and the league's comeback player of the year award.

8. *Maurice Greene Becomes Fastest Man in World*

He often said it was a dream of his — since childhood, really — to become the "fastest man in the world." While other track stars might have had that same dream, Maurice Greene lived it. With motivation of missing the 1996 Olympics in Atlanta after suffering a hamstring injury during the trials, Greene set his sights on the 2000 Games.

In the fall of 1996, Greene moved from his home in Kansas City, Kansas, and headed to Los Angeles to train under John Smith. Greene started realizing his childhood dream the next year, when he won the 100 meters at the World Championships with a record-tying time of 9.86 seconds. Although some contend that's when Greene laid claim to the moniker "fastest man in the world," traditionally, the person with that title comes out of the Olympics. Still, Greene won the 100 meters at the 1999 World Championships in Seville, Spain, with a time of 9.80.

One year later, Greene reached his ultimate goal at the 2000 Games in Sydney. Greene jumped out to a quick start and beat one of his training partners, Ato Boldon, with a time of 9.87. He had now legitimately earned the right to call himself the "fastest man in the world."

7. *Frank White Captures 8th Gold Glove Award, 1987*

The title of his instructional book couldn't be more appropriate: *Good As Gold*. After all, if anyone knows a thing or two or eight about gold, it's Frank White, the possessor of eight Gold Glove Awards from his storied career at second base for the Royals.

Frank White

White won his first six during 1977-82, and then back-to-back, 1986-87. During the season in which he claimed his last Gold Glove, White committed 10 errors and finished with a .987 fielding percentage.

Although biased, many Royals fans felt that White should've received his ninth Gold Glove in 1988 when he committed just four errors — all throwing errors — and led the league in fielding percentage at .994. Instead, the award went to Seattle's Harold Reynolds, who had one of his worst defensive seasons with 18 errors and a .977 fielding percentage. White's eighth Gold Glove set a record for American League second basemen. He remains one of only four second basemen in the history of the game to reach eight, along with Bill Mazeroski (8), Ryne Sandberg (9) and Roberto Alomar (10).

During his 18-year career, White committed 206 errors en route to a lifetime .983 fielding percentage.

6. *Tom Watson Wins 1982 U.S. Open*

"What can you say? Tom Watson, pitching into the hole for a birdie, has taken the lead in the U.S. Open. One more par and he's finally won it!"
— Jim McKay's call on ABC after Watson birdied 17 from the rough

Jack Nicklaus knew all about the long par-three 17th hole at Pebble Beach, site of the 1982 U.S. Open. After all, he delivered one of the U.S. Open's most famous shots exactly a decade earlier on the famous hole surrounded by the Pacific Ocean and weeds. That year, using a one-iron, Nicklaus struck the ball as a gust of wind came off the water. His shot hit the flag and landed less than six inches from the cup. He birdied the hole and ended with a three-stroke Open win.

So, when Nicklaus, sitting in the scorer's tent tied for the lead with Tom Watson at four-under, saw that Watson hit his tee shot into the high rough to the left of the 17th green, he felt a little confident. And, why not? To get in position to get his record fifth U.S. Open title, Nicklaus birdied five straight holes early in the final round. He took a one-stroke lead over previous co-leaders Watson and Bill Rogers, who were playing three groups behind him. As the back nine holes played out, Rogers faded quickly. The lead went back and forth between Nicklaus and Watson, who held it by a stroke until he bogeyed 16 with Nicklaus finished for the day. Then, Watson took what appeared to be the disastrous shot on 17.

As Watson studied his predicament, his caddie Bruce Edwards, trying to stay positive, told Watson to "get it close."

"I'm not going to get it close," Watson replied, "I'm going to make it."

Watson later explained his apparent confidence. "I knew that was my only real chance to get the ball anyplace close to the hole was to hit the flagstick," he said. "No matter how soft I landed it, if it didn't hit the stick, it was going to pick up speed and go at least ten or fifteen feet, maybe more, past the hole. ... But when I stood over the ball, I was absolutely trying to make it. It was my best chance."

Watson took two practice swings, slightly moved the club in his fingertips and took the shot. The ball landed a few inches inside the fringe, took a small bounce, rolled directly into the stick, and dropped into the hole. When it was just inches from the hole, Watson began his now famous trot around the green with a relieved grin on his face.

"It was just instinct," Watson, who normally doesn't show emotion on the course, said of his reaction. "It was a miraculous shot and it gave me a one-shot lead with one hole to play in the Open. So I celebrated more than I normally do."

Watson birdied 18 and closed out one of the most remarkable days the U.S. Open had seen before or since.

5. *The Slipper Fits KU in 1988*

It's easy to understand why Kansas fans never tire of talking about 1988. In appreciation for the city and famed Municipal Auditorium hosting more tournament games (83) than any other venue, and more national championship games (9) than any other arena in the country, the NCAA gave Kansas City a gift in the form of allowing it to play host to the 50th anniversary of the championship. University of Kansas fans received a bigger gift with "Danny and the Miracles" and the magical run to the national championship at Kemper Arena. In spite of the team's 11 losses throughout the year, Kansas received an invitation to the "Big Dance" as a sixth-seeded at-large team.

The Jayhawks took care of Duke in the semifinal game before facing then-Big Eight rival Oklahoma in the championship. In spite of OU's dominance over Kansas during the regular season, winning both contests, Danny Manning and his teammates played with the Sooners in the first half, tying the 50th anniversary of the championship at 50-50.

"Who knows, maybe the 1988 Kansas team was one of destiny," said long-time KU radio announcer Bob Davis. "The last three losses the Jayhawks suffered during the season were to Duke, Oklahoma and Kansas State (in the Big Eight Tournament). The last three wins of the season for Kansas, interestingly enough, were against Kansas State (NCAA Tournament Midwest Regional Final), Duke and Oklahoma."

Manning finished KU's 83-79 win over Oklahoma with 31 points and 18 rebounds, while the Jayhawks shot nearly 71 percent from the field.

(*Editor's Note: See feature article on game in Chapter 12*)

4. *Royals Sweep Yankees in 1980 ALCS*

This had been a long time coming. Too long, in fact. For the fourth time in five seasons, the Yankees stood between the Royals and the World Series. This time, though, the Royals had the relief pitcher they had so desperately needed in the previous three series, and they got a little extra boost from their Hall-of-Fame third baseman.

After the Royals took the first two games in the best-of-five American League Championship Series at home, the teams headed to the Bronx. In the top of the fifth inning, Frank White put the Royals ahead with a solo home run off New York starter Tommy John. With one out in the bottom of the sixth, New York's Reggie Jackson doubled off Royals starter Paul Splittorff. Manager Jim Frey brought in closer Dan Quisenberry, who gave up RBI singles to Oscar Gamble and Rick Cerone, and the Yankees took a 2-1 lead.

But, in the top of the seventh, U.L. Washington beat out an infield single with Willie Wilson aboard and two outs. Then, George Brett, who was the game's best hitter in 1980, stepped up to the plate to face baseball's most intimidating reliever, Rich "Goose" Gossage. His first pitch was a fastball down the middle. Brett responded by sending the ball into the upper deck, giving the Royals a 4-2 lead.

"The noise. ... The noise of the bat, the sound of the bat — it was like nothing I had ever heard before," Gossage said. "It was the loudest crack. I will never forget that crack. And then the silence."

Quisenberry pitched himself and the Royals out of a pickle in the eighth inning after giving up a triple to Bob Watson and then walking Jackson and Gamble. A double play and a groundout later, the Royals escaped and went on to win the game and sweep the Yankees.

"I remember running back toward the infield for the celebration," said John Wathan, who was playing right in the ninth inning when Quiz struck out Willie Randolph for the final out. "It was the only time in my whole career that I cried on the field. It almost felt like we were world champs already."

3. Chiefs Win Super Bowl IV

In case you missed the feature article on the game earlier in this chapter, here's a recap: the Chiefs beat the Minnesota Vikings 23-7 in the final AFL-NFL Championship game, or what's known today as Super Bowl IV.

2. Joe Montana Leads Chiefs past John Elway and the Broncos on MNF

Chiefs fans had seen this before — five times over the previous five years — Denver quarterback John Elway leading the Broncos down the field for a game-winning drive in the closing minutes. And, he did it again in 1994, except for the whole game-winning part. This Monday Night Football match-up belonged to another Hall of Fame quarterback known for his late-game heroics: Joe Montana.

As expected, Elway led the Broncos to a touchdown and their first lead of the game, 28-24, with 1:29 to play in the fourth quarter. Needing a touchdown, that's not enough time for normal quarterbacks. But it was too much time for Montana, who was anything but an "average Joe."

Montana, whose status for the game was questionable because of a bruised hip, definitely didn't seem too injured as he drove the Chiefs 75 yards on 7-of-8 passing, including a couple of runs by another Hall of Famer, Marcus Allen. From Denver's 5-yard-line, Montana found wide receiver Willie Davis, who squeaked in at the front corner of the end zone for the winning touchdown with eight seconds left. Chiefs 31, Broncos 28.

1. *Royals Win 1985 World Series*

1985 Royals World Series Trophy

Even though the St. Louis Cardinals seemed to be the favorite to win the 1985 World Series, and proved their dominance by taking a 3-games-to-1 advantage in the Series against the Royals, Kansas City battled back for its first-ever world championship. The Royals, featuring a young and relatively inexperienced pitching staff surrounded on the field by a perfect mix of youth, veterans and doggedness, came back from series deficits of 2-0 and 3-1 in both the American League playoffs against Toronto and the World Series against the Cards.

(Editor's Note: See feature article in Chapter 1)

KANSAS CITY'S BIGGEST SPORTS LOSSES

10. *Chiefs Lose to Green Bay 35-10 in Super Bowl I*

Since its inception in 1960, its brethren in the National Football League had looked down upon the American Football League. Many observers saw the AFL as a "Mickey Mouse" league. After the 1966 season, the two leagues sent their best to Los Angeles to see which was best in what's now known as Super Bowl I. As one might imagine, a tremendous amount of pride was on the line for both sides. The teams of the NFL looked upon the Green Bay Packers to uphold the tradition and "superiority" of their league. The Chiefs hoped to disprove that idea and show they deserved to be on the same field with the Packers.

The Chiefs kept the game close in the first half. They matched a Bart Starr to Max McGee touchdown with a Len Dawson to Curtis McClinton scoring play, and then got a field goal from Mike Mercer just before halftime after another Green Bay touchdown. Despite that 14-10 score coming out of the intermission, Kansas City couldn't slow down the Packer offense in the second half. Possibly the biggest play of the game came in the third quarter when Green Bay's Willie Wood intercepted a pass attempt from Dawson to Fred Arbanas, and ran it back to the Chiefs 5. The Packers scored during their next series and didn't look back.

"That was such an emotional game because we knew the importance of it since we were competing with the NFL," said E.J. Holub, who played center and linebacker during his 10-year career with the Texans and Chiefs. "We made mistakes because we were overexcited. We got burned."

9. *Royals Lose to Yankees in Game 5 of 1977 ALCS*

It was the best team in franchise history, winning 102 games. During one stretch in 1977, the Royals won 24 of 25 games. After losing to the Yankees in the fifth game of the 1976 playoffs, the Royals carried confidence throughout the '77 ALCS, splitting the first two games in New York before coming back to Kansas City to win Game 3. Even after the Yankees won the fourth game, the Royals came out fighting in Game 5...literally.

George Brett slid into third with the club's trademark aggressive style in the first inning, sparking a brawl at the base with Yankee third baseman Graig Nettles. After scoring two runs in that first, the Royals held a lead until the ninth inning.

Thin in the bullpen, manager Whitey Herzog brought in Dennis Leonard, winner of Game 3, to record the final three outs. It didn't happen. Through a couple dink hits, a walk and a throwing error by Brett, the Yankees scored three runs in the top of the inning and held off the Royals in the bottom half to win 5-3.

"Even though we won three pennants and a World Series in St. Louis," said Herzog, "the 1977 Royals team was the best team I ever managed. We had the Yankees down two games to one. That was a playoff we should have won."

8. *MU 5th Down Loss to Colorado, October 6, 1990*

It's one thing to lose a close game that you aren't expected to win anyway. It's quite another to have that victory taken from you because of an officiating blunder. Just ask the Missouri Tigers.

In a series that still pains the hearts of Missouri fans, the eventual co-national champion Colorado Buffaloes got a little extra help in their come-from-behind victory against the Tigers in Columbia in October 1990.

The Tigers led 31-27 when Colorado got a first down at Missouri's 3-yard line in the final minute of the fourth quarter. Buffalo quarterback Charles Johnson quickly got under center and spiked the ball with 31 seconds left. Second down.

On the next play, Eric Bieniemy ran up the middle, good for two yards. Colorado called its final timeout with 18 seconds left. Third down.

After the timeout, Bieniemy again tried to go up the middle, but was stopped. Officials called a timeout to get the ball set with 8 seconds remaining. Fourth down.

Johnson again spiked the ball. Fifth down.

With two seconds left, Johnson kept the ball on the next play and reached out over the right side. Touchdown. Victory to Colorado. Stunned Tiger fans.

"The Fifth Down game was more eerie than gut-wrenching," life-long Missouri fan Brad Doolittle wrote in an email for this book. "Mizzou was not very good that year, for one thing. And something seemed out of sorts at the end but nobody knew what. Everyone stood around for a good five minutes after the game because it just seemed like they needed to keep playing. Gradually word started to get around what had happened and then it was really bad."

In the end, it was determined that the officials failed to change the down marker to third down the first time around. Although there's no telling what would've happened if the markers were correct, one thing is for sure: Colorado went on to win the Big Eight and the Orange Bowl, and with its undefeated record, claimed a share of the national championship with Georgia Tech.

7. *North Carolina Beats Kansas in Triple Overtime for 1957 National Championship*

The Kansas Jayhawks headed into the 1957 national title game at Kansas City's Municipal Auditorium against North Carolina as the first team in NCAA history to reach the finals four times. And they did so as the favorite. That doesn't seem like a big deal, except the Tar Heels were the top-ranked team in the country.

"It might be the only time in history that the undefeated number-one team in the nation went into the championship game as the underdog," said Lennie Rosenbluth, North Carolina's leading scorer that season. There's one reason for the Jayhawks' popularity: Wilt Chamberlain.

"The 1957 season was one in which the Kansas Jayhawks would have been considered a failure if they did not win the national championship," legendary radio announcer Max Falkenstien wrote in the book, *CBS Sports Presents: Stories from the Final Four.*

Carolina head coach Frank McGuire, a master tactician and psychologist, felt his team would win if it forced every Jayhawk not named Chamberlain to make plays. As for the head games, he started that immediately by jumping 5-foot-10 Tommy Kearns against the imposing Chamberlain. Carolina jumped out to an early lead and controlled the game's tempo.

After regulation and two overtime periods during which each team had its chances, the game came down to the final play of the third overtime. The Tar Heels led 54-53 with 6 seconds left. After a KU timeout, as expected, the Jayhawks tried to get the ball to Chamberlain, but Joe Quigg, who hit two free throws that gave North Carolina the lead, tipped Ron Loneski's pass. Game over.

"The loss was difficult for the Kansas players and coaches, but it may have been toughest on Wilt," wrote Falkenstien. "The pressure placed on him throughout the season made him feel as though he let the team, and Kansas fans, down by not leading them to the title."

6. *Chiefs "Monday Night Meltdown," November 16, 1998*

Ugly. That's the only word to describe the Chiefs' 30-7 loss at Arrowhead against Denver on Monday Night Football. Well, maybe not the only word. There's embarrassing, disgraceful, shameful, appalling, and dreadful. OK, there are several ways to describe the game. Although no loss to Denver is acceptable to any self-respecting Chiefs fan, this one was magnified by actions on the field.

The Chiefs were flagged for five personal fouls — including three straight by Derrick Thomas, who evidently let the smack-talking Shannon Sharpe get under his skin — all during an 80-yard Denver touchdown drive in the fourth quarter.

"My actions were uncharacteristic and in some sense uncalled for," Thomas said during an apology the day after the game, when the Chiefs announced that they suspended him for one game. "Being one of the individuals everybody looks up to on this football team, I have to conduct myself in a manner that is positive at all times."

The "Monday Night Meltdown" marked the Chiefs' fifth loss in a row. They'd go on to lose the next week. Following the season, after his team's disappointing 7-9 finish, coach Marty Schottenheimer resigned.

5. *Kings Leave Kansas City, 1985*

Were you one of the few who claims you were there? Oh, saying that you were there might not carry the same magnitude as telling someone you were at the Chiefs-Dolphins Christmas Day game, or the KU-OU national championship game in 1988, or either Game 6 or 7 of the 1985 World Series. But in terms of significance to the history of sports here, it's something if you can say that you were at the Kansas City Kings game on April 14, 1985. If you were at Kemper Arena that day, witnessing the final game for the Kings in Kansas City, a loss to the Los Angeles Lakers, you weren't alone — well, not completely alone. With the assumption that the Kings were moving to Sacramento, 11,371 fans showed up, which was about 7,000 more than the team had been drawing that season.

"It's exciting to think you're going to go someplace better. We thought we'd play in front of sell out crowds (in Sacramento). That was the only positive to me," said Eddie Johnson, who enjoyed his best NBA season in 1984-85 by leading the Kings with 22.9 points per game. "Most athletes, if they look back at their career and see what moves helped and hurt them, our move to Sacramento hurt me."

It wasn't all that good for Kansas City, either.

The Kings came to Kansas City, bringing NBA basketball for the first time, in 1972. For their first three seasons after leaving Cincinnati where they were called the Royals, the Kings split "home" time between K.C. and Omaha.

"Omaha took a lot out of us," said legendary Kings player Sam Lacey, who spent two seasons in Cincinnati, all three in Kansas City-Omaha and then six-plus years in Kansas City. "There were many days that we'd get in (to Kansas City from Omaha) at 6:00 and go straight to the arena to play our game that night."

The Kings' time in Kansas City was marked by team mediocrity in spite of great players. During the organization's 10 seasons in Kansas City, the Kings reached the playoffs four times and finished only four seasons with a record above the .500 mark. (In 1983, they finished with a 45-37 record and didn't make the playoffs. The next season, their record was 38-44 but they did make the playoffs.)

Before the start of the 1983-84 season, a group of Sacramento investors bought the team for cash, plus its $10.5 million in debts. Two days after the Kings lost to the Lakers, on April 16, 1985, the NBA Board of Governors voted unanimously to allow the Kings to move to Sacramento.

4. "Mr. K" Passes Away

Baseball in Kansas City hasn't been the same since one of the saddest days in the city's sports history: August 1, 1993, the day Ewing Kauffman, the founder and owner of the Royals, passed away after a battle with cancer. He was 76.

Although he was best known as the Royals' owner, "Mr. K" was also a self-made billionaire and one of the city's best philanthropists. There's no telling how many people Kauffman touched through his community service and his ball club. Among his ventures was PROJECT CHOICE, which gave students at Westport High School, Kauffman's alma mater, a chance to attend college on Kauffman's dime — if they graduated high school and stayed out of trouble.

"I learned (from Kauffman) that it isn't stupid to reward people, and it isn't stupid to pay people, it isn't stupid to share," said Barnett Helzberg, another icon in business and the Kansas City community.

Kauffman always tried to reward his players, too. For instance, if the team was going through a losing streak and Mr. K felt they needed a pick-me-up, it was common for him to go into the clubhouse after a game and hand each player a $100 bill and say, "Take your wife to dinner tonight." (With the exception of times like those, Mr. K was a behind-the-scenes owner.)

Then there's his idea for the Royals Baseball Academy, which tried to mold great athletes into baseball players while helping them get an education. It was short-lived, but productive in the club's history.

"Mr. K was a special man, not only to Kansas City but to me," said Royals Hall of Fame second baseman and nearly life-long Kansas Citian Frank White, who is the greatest success story from the Academy. "If it hadn't been for Mr. Kauffman, I wouldn't have been in baseball. ... He was very community minded and he knew that Kansas City needed baseball, so he worked hard to purchase the new franchise. He stuck with the club during the lean times, and he rewarded players with a chance to play championship baseball and the city of Kansas City to see championship baseball."

When Kauffman purchased the Royals, he wasn't a big baseball fan. But, he loved Kansas City and felt the fans needed major-league baseball. During the year leading up to his death, Kauffman, now the Royals' biggest fan, helped ensure that a plan was in place to find a suitable owner for the Royals and keep the club in Kansas City.

Appropriately, at the end of his private funeral on August 4, an organist played "Take Me Out to the Ballgame" as they carried Mr. K's casket out of the church.

3. Chiefs Lose to Buffalo 30-13 in AFC Championship, January 23, 1994

Buffalo had been there the previous three years. And won all three, only to lose in all three trips to the Super Bowl. The Chiefs hadn't advanced this far since Super Bowl IV, 24 years earlier. Buffalo's experience, along with a powerful running game, ended the Chiefs dreams of going to the Super Bowl behind future Hall of Famers Joe Montana and Marcus Allen.

Buffalo took an early 7-0 lead and never trailed, as Bills' running back Thurman Thomas racked up 186 yards and three touchdowns on 33 carries, along with 22 receiving yards. (The Bills rushed for 229 yards while holding the Chiefs to 52.) The Chiefs had a chance to cut into Buffalo's 20-6 lead before halftime, but with 21 seconds remaining, Montana threw an interception in the end zone. To make matters worse, Montana suffered a concussion on the third play of the third quarter and didn't return to the game. Back-up quarterback Dave Krieg led the Chiefs to their lone touchdown of the game, a 90-yard scoring drive late in the third quarter that ended with a 1-yard touchdown dive by Allen.

2. *Yankees Beat Royals in Game 5 of the 1976 ALCS*

The Royals reached their first-ever postseason in 1976 and sparked what turned out to be a long and often frustrating rivalry with the New York Yankees. The best-of-five games series was knotted at two games each heading into the finale at Yankee Stadium on October 14, 1976. With the scored tied 6-6 in the bottom of the ninth, Royals manager Whitey Herzog brought in relief pitcher Mark Littell to face Chris Chambliss.

"On paper, this was a classic match-up," broadcaster Denny Matthews wrote in *Play by Play*, the book he co-authored with long-time partner Fred White. "Littell had (given up one) home run during the 1976 season. Chambliss had teed off for a homer in the third game of the series to help give the Yankees the win in that contest."

After about a 5-minute delay to clean up trash that Yankee fans had thrown onto the field, mainly in right field, Littell, the fifth Royals pitcher of the game, got set. Chambliss sent the first pitch over the outstretched glove of right fielder Hal McRae and over the fence. The ball made it over McRae's glove by a dog's hair.

To play the "what-if" game for a moment, there's an interesting side note that's often forgotten. Al Cowens, the Royals regular right fielder, was playing center because Amos Otis hurt his ankle early in the first game.

"We lost that series on the first play of the first game, when Otis broke his ankle," Herzog said in the book *Moments, Memories, Miracles* by Steve Cameron. "Not only did we miss his bat, but I had to move Cowens to center field and put McRae in right. When Chambliss hit that ball off Mark Littell, it probably only cleared Hal's glove by an inch. Cowens is six inches taller. He'd have caught it. That's how close we came."

1. *Chiefs Lose to Miami 27-24 on Christmas Day, 1971*

It has been termed pro football's longest day. Eighty-two minutes, 40 seconds. And one of the best games in NFL history. For Kansas City fans, it's simply the worst loss. Playing host to a Miami Dolphins team that was a season away from undefeated immortality, the Chiefs got a playoff record 350 all-purpose yards from Ed Podolak during the double-overtime game. But it wasn't enough.

Although it's unfair to place the blame for the Chiefs losing this incredible contest, the normally sure-footed Jan Stenerud often has laid the guilt on his own shoulders. Stenerud missed two field-goal attempts, including a 31-yarder at the end of regulation that sailed a few inches too far to the right.

"I think about the game all the time," Stenerud said in Joe McGuff's column in *The Kansas City Star* 11 days later. "It's bad enough letting the fans down, but the thing that bugs me is letting down the players and the coaches. I didn't really come through in the clutch."

Another attempt, this one from 42 yards during overtime, was blocked.

Eventually, Miami kicker Garo Yepremian ended the game with a 37-yard field goal.

"That was our best team during my time in Kansas City," said Jim Kearney, who played for the Chiefs during 1967-75 without ever missing a game due to an injury. "The Miami Dolphins won the Super Bowl that year, but we had a better team. ... I cannot remember driving home from that old stadium after that game. It's like a *Twilight Zone*. I guess it was denial."

"Most of us, including those on the (Super Bowl IV) team, felt that the '71 team was better," said Podolak. "We finished the season very strong and felt that we could go all the way again. That game was the beginning of the dominance of the Miami Dolphins and the beginning of the fade of the Kansas City Chiefs."

Indeed. The Chiefs didn't return to the playoffs until 1986. The Christmas Day game also was the team's final one at Municipal Stadium. They moved to Arrowhead the next season.

BASEBALL
in
KANSAS CITY

Chapter 3

Buck O'Neil:
Life of a Legend

A smile creeps across Bob Kendrick's face. He's thinking about the first time he realized the magnitude of John Jordan "Buck" O'Neil. It's a story that Kendrick has told countless times about his "94-year-old partner and buddy." Regardless how often he's recalled it, the awe remains in his voice. The moment happened during FanFest at the 2001 All-Star Game in Seattle.

"Buck and I were walking toward the Negro Leagues exhibit and there was a white gentleman we didn't know," Kendrick, the Marketing Director for the Negro Leagues Baseball Museum, remembered on October 5, 2006, the day before O'Neil passed away.

"This gentleman was standing next to a picture of Buck. When he saw the real Buck walk in, uncontrollable tears started rolling down his face. He was so honored to meet Buck. I just kept thinking, 'Wow!' I think it even stunned Buck to see that kind of reaction from someone who had dreamed of meeting him.

"But Buck was typical Buck. He shook hands, took pictures and talked with the gentleman. It was such a surreal moment for that gentleman. And, at that moment, it was etched in my mind just how big Buck really was."

♦ ♦ ♦

It's about an hour before an early-season Royals game in April 2005. John "Buck" O'Neil, decked out in a suit and tie, complete with a fedora, saunters behind the batting cage. Players and coaches from both clubs stop and talk with O'Neil. Of course, he offers a couple nuggets of wisdom when he can. Or, at the very least, a tale from his days in the Negro Leagues.

But this is it. It's the reason he can saunter. Another baseball season is in full swing at Kauffman Stadium. Buck's home. Really, though, *any* ballpark is home to Buck O'Neil. That's what happens when you've been around professional baseball for 70 years.

For the majority of those seven decades, O'Neil had been in the Kansas City area, most notably as a first baseman and then a manager with the Kansas City Monarchs during 1938-55. It was a good time to be a Monarch.

"The Monarchs were more or less like the great Yankee ball clubs," said O'Neil, whose mind was as sharp as ever at 93 years old. "Any white kid wanted to play with the Yankees. Any black kid wanted to play for the Monarchs. So we got some of the best players out there."

That also was a great time to be a baseball star in Kansas City.

"Kansas City was a very exciting city," said O'Neil, who first called Kansas City home in 1946. "People liked baseball. They always filled up the ballpark.

"It also was a great place for musicians. They could get a gig here and people would flock here. That's when I met guys like Count Basie and Duke Ellington, and all of those guys. Man, 18th and Vine was jumping."

Just a few blocks away, O'Neil played with some of baseball's best at the old Muehlebach Field (which became Municipal Stadium, the home of the A's and the original home of the Royals). There were Hall of Famers Satchel Paige, Hilton Smith, Bullet Joe Rogan and Turkey Stearnes, plus other greats such as Willie Brown and Ted Strong.

The team was especially tough during the 1942 season, a club that O'Neil calls the greatest during his time with the Monarchs.

"Everybody was a star at his position on that ballclub. These guys were superstars, really," O'Neil said. "They could do it all — hit, run, field, throw."

And they did it all during the 1942 Negro World Series, against the favored Homestead Grays, a team that had won all four of their head-to-head meetings that season. The Grays featured the likes of Josh Gibson and Buck Leonard.

48

The Negro World Series was played in several cities each year, so more African-Americans could see the games. After beating the Grays in the first two games in Washington, D.C., the Monarchs and Grays moved to Yankee Stadium in front of 30,000 people for the next contest. The Monarchs cruised to a 9-3 win.

In the fourth game, at Philadelphia's Shibe Park, O'Neil had three hits, including an inside-the-park homer. The Monarchs swept the Homestead Grays, four games to none.

"We just had an excellent baseball team that year," said O'Neil, who batted .353 during those four games. "To make a baseball team, and I don't care how many superstars you have on a ball club, until you mold them into a team, they don't win. Our superstars were a team, and we won."

Despite O'Neil's three-hit performance in the clinching game, his greatest moment as a player came a few months later, on Easter Sunday, 1943.

The Monarchs opened the season in Memphis against their Negro American League rival Red Sox. In his first three plate appearances, O'Neil doubled, singled and homered, respectively. He came up to bat again late in the game.

"I hit it to left-center, and it looked like it was going out of the ballpark," remembered O'Neil. "As I was going to first I was thinking, 'Hit the fence, hit the fence.' Sure enough, the ball hit the fence and bounced back between the center fielder and left fielder. When I got to third base, the coach was calling me to go home for an inside-the-park home run. But I stopped at third. I wanted that triple. And I got the cycle."

More importantly, that also happened to be one of Buck O'Neil's best days off the field.

"That night, I was in the hotel relaxing when 'Dizzy' Dismukes, our traveling secretary, called my room and said, 'Buck, I want you to come downstairs. There are some people I want you to meet,'" O'Neil said. "The wife of the man that ran the restaurant in the hotel was a schoolteacher, and she had invited some young schoolteachers over to the hotel to meet the ballplayers. When I got downstairs, these people were sitting in front of the door. I walked straight over to a young woman and said, 'My name's Buck O'Neil.'"

Her name was Ora.

"We were married for 51 years. Easter Sunday, 1943, Memphis, Tennessee. I hit for the cycle and met my future wife. That was my greatest day in baseball."

Although O'Neil was a solid first baseman, he was known more as an offensive player. During his 12-year career, which included three trips to the East-West All-Star Game, he batted .288. O'Neil hit a career-high .358 in 1947, and won two batting titles, in 1940 and '46.

From 1948-55, O'Neil managed the Monarchs, leading the club to four league championships. He also managed the West squad in the All-Star Game four times, winning each contest.

It stood to reason then that O'Neil could recognize talent when he saw it. The Chicago Cubs hired him in 1956 to do just that as a scout. They weren't disappointed.

"I signed Ernie Banks, Lou Brock, Joe Carter and Lee Arthur Smith," O'Neil said proudly of his star players. "The first two are Hall of Famers and the next two are future Hall of Famers."

Besides the great players O'Neil signed, he made a significant contribution to baseball during his 32-year career with the Cubs when, in 1962, he became the first African-American coach in the major leagues.

In 1988, the same year O'Neil retired from the Cubs, then-Royals General Manager John Schuerholz offered O'Neil a job as special assignment scout. He was associated with the club from that moment on.

"The job with the Royals turned out to be even more rewarding than I expected," O'Neil wrote in his book, *I Was Right On Time.*

Oddly enough, while O'Neil was at Kauffman Stadium scouting American League teams for the Cubs, he first saw a young player whom he later got to know while working for the Royals: Bo Jackson.

"In my era, the best athletes in the world were baseball players," O'Neil said. "Football and basketball were more or less college sports. So the best white athlete in the world played Major League Baseball. The best black athlete in the world played Negro League Baseball.

"All of that has changed now. We don't necessarily get the best athlete in the world anymore in baseball."

"I believe today's (baseball players) are bigger, stronger and faster," he added. "But the last *great* athlete we've had in baseball is Bo Jackson."

If anyone should know, it's Buck O'Neil. After all, during his tenure in professional baseball, he was around the game's best. Think about it: in more than 70 years, O'Neil played and managed with or against, and scouted most of baseball's magnificent players.

He played against Babe Ruth and Josh Gibson and Buck Leonard. He played with Satchel Paige and Hilton Smith. And the list goes on and on.

"The best Major League ballplayer I ever saw was Willie Mays," O'Neil said without hesitation. "Ruth beat you with the bat. Ted Williams beat you with the bat. Joe DiMaggio beat you with the bat, his glove and his arm. But Willie Mays could beat you with the bat, with power, his glove, his arm and with the running. He could beat you any way that's possible."

That doesn't mean Mays was O'Neil's choice for the greatest ever to lace up the spikes.

"The best ballplayer I ever saw," he said, "was Oscar Charleston, who didn't play in the Major Leagues. Oscar played centerfield (in the Negro Leagues). He could hit 50 home runs and steal 50 bases in a season, and that was during the deadball era.

"People compare players today to Willie Mays, but we old-timers say Willie Mays was the closest thing to Oscar Charleston."

For 15 years, visitors could regularly find Buck O'Neil reliving stories of Charleston and Mays and Satchel at the Negro Leagues Baseball Museum in the renovated 18th and Vine district. He loved sharing the story of the Negro Leagues and all of baseball's great players with anyone who would listen.

Of course, everyone listened.

"Baseball's been my life," he said. "I made my living in baseball for 70 years. Really, I've met some wonderful, wonderful people in baseball."

◆ ◆ ◆

With Major League Baseball players and owners going through the 1994 strike that eventually wiped out the World Series, fans needed their fall fix. They got it in September, thanks to documentary filmmaker Ken Burns and his PBS series *Baseball*. The "nine-inning" documentary gave fans a nightly escape for two weeks from Donald Fehr, Richard Ravitch and Bud Selig.

Within the documentary, in "Inning 5: Shadow Ball," there was this captivating storyteller, offering anecdotes of Satchel Paige and Josh Gibson and other Negro League players that even the die-hardest of the die-hard, "seam-head" baseball fans hadn't heard. The storyteller was, of course, Buck O'Neil.

Literally overnight, O'Neil, at 82 years old, became a national celebrity.

"Buck had this mistaken assumption that we who had made the series on baseball were somehow responsible for his celebrity," Burns said during the memorial service for O'Neil at Municipal Auditorium on October 14, 2006. "I had always argued the opposite; that we had merely plugged in an amplifier, that it was in fact Buck who was responsible for our success. He wouldn't hear of it, and this became an ongoing thing between us."

Either way, the timing couldn't have been better for O'Neil and the Negro Leagues Baseball Museum, and baseball overall in Kansas City.

There's certainly an interesting coincidence for baseball fans in Kansas City that O'Neil's rise in popularity occurred at a time when the Royals were in the midst of a steady decline on the field.

The 1994 season, the Royals' first in the AL Central, saw the club make a serious push in the division for only the third time since winning the 1985 World Series. When the 1994 strike hit, the Royals were 13 games above .500. The closest they've come to finishing that well was in 2003 when they concluded the season with a record of 83-79.

Meanwhile, Buck O'Neil's popularity skyrocketed since '94, both locally and nationally. In spite of the Royals struggles, O'Neil gave sports fans and the city a consistently positive baseball story.

Although many Kansas Citians feel as though O'Neil has been a local icon for generations, that's not actually the case. Truth told, it took the Burns' *Baseball* series to bring O'Neil and the Negro Leagues to the mainstream, even in Kansas City, the birthplace of the Negro National League in 1920.

Baseball, along with the Major League work stoppage, put a tremendous light on the Negro Leagues Baseball Museum, O'Neil's greatest legacy to date. After all, he was instrumental in the birth of the museum that opened in 1991 in a small one-room office.

Horace Peterson III, who was the head of the black archives in Kansas City, called O'Neil with the idea of forming a Negro Leagues Hall of Fame.

O'Neil responded adamantly with a different idea: "I said, 'No, we don't need a Hall of Fame because I think the guys who are qualified should be in the Hall of Fame in Cooperstown. There has been enough separation in baseball. We should have a Negro Leagues Baseball Museum.'"

"Former Monarchs paid the rent — I paid it one month, Lefty LaMarque paid it one month, Connie Johnson paid it one month, and so on," O'Neil added during an interview in 2005. "That's the way we existed until Reverend Emanuel Cleaver, who was a Councilman at the time, got money for (the 18th and Vine) area."

In 1994, the same year as *Burns' Baseball*, the NLBM moved from the one-room office to a 2,000 square-foot facility. Then, in 1997, the Negro Leagues and Jazz museums moved into a 50,000 square-foot building.

"It's not really possible to put into words (what Buck's meant to the NLBM) because, in many respects, he has become the face of the Negro Leagues," said Bob Kendrick. "He has made many people around this country care about and want to learn more about the Negro Leagues. Obviously, he has been the man who sculpted this organization into the great museum that it has become. He did it with unbridled energy, passion, and gave tirelessly of his own time over the last 16 years to build this institution.

"Obviously there are a lot of people involved in building this museum, but this museum does not happen without the work of Buck O'Neil. No ifs, ands, buts or maybes about that. He's meant that much to this organization."

In 2006, O'Neil gained a new passion when the Museum started a "Thanks a Million, Buck" campaign to build the Buck O'Neil Education and Research Center, which will be housed in a renovated Paseo YMCA, the very building where "Rube" Foster founded the Negro National League in 1920.

"With Buck's education and resource center, we can take (the Negro Leagues) history and practically apply it to what's happening in lives today, particularly in the lives of young people," Kendrick said. "And we'll make it interactive so they're not just reading about history for history's sake. Hopefully we can be cutting-edge in our thinking of how we get this message out."

The Buck O'Neil Education and Research Center will be much, much more than a stuffy research library, though.

The facility, which is an expansion of the Negro Leagues Baseball Museum, will include expanded exhibit spaces to house new artifacts; classrooms where people can learn, for instance, about the math and science of baseball; an interactive baseball experience; a formal baseball training facility, where urban kids can get year-round baseball training; and a technology center, where people living around the 18th and Vine district can keep up with technological advances.

Said Kendrick: "We'd be doing, in essence, what Negro Leagues Baseball did in communities across the country in its hey-day — be an economic stimulus and provide leadership in the community."

And, the Negro Leagues Baseball Museum would be doing what Buck O'Neil had been doing for decades — keeping the league's history alive — but finally became heard, thanks to Ken Burns, PBS and the baseball strike of '94.

◆ ◆ ◆

It had been a long year, 2006. There was the disappointment early in the year felt by Buck O'Neil and all of his fans when a special committee selecting players from the Negro Leagues for inclusion in the Baseball Hall of Fame inexplicably passed over O'Neil.

Then there was the full appearance schedule. With his trademark smile and unbridled enthusiasm, Buck traveled the country throughout the year with a mobile Negro Leagues exhibit. He also fit in every speaking engagement that he could.

During an incredibly hot spell late in the summer, he appeared at an old-timer's game the night before his highly publicized appearance in the Independent Northern League All-Star Game in Kansas City, Kansas. Finally, the summer culminated with O'Neil's Hall of Fame acceptance speech on behalf of the Negro League players that he helped enshrine.

The physical and mental strain of such a hectic year would have been difficult for anyone. Especially so, though, for someone at the age of 94.

A few days after returning to Kansas City from Cooperstown, Buck checked himself into a hospital. He didn't feel right; he was worn out. A few weeks after that short stay, he returned to the hospital.

On Friday night, October 6, 2006, O'Neil passed away. He was a month away from his 95th birthday.

"Major League Baseball is saddened by the passing of Buck O'Neil," MLB Commissioner Bud Selig said through a written statement. "Buck was a pioneer, a legend who will be missed for as long as the game is played. I had the good fortune of spending some time with him in Cooperstown a couple of months ago and I will miss his wisdom and counsel."

Indeed, with the passing of John "Buck" O'Neil, the game lost its greatest living link between the Negro Leagues and Major League Baseball. Kansas City, however, lost one of its greatest ambassadors and its most beloved legend.

♦ ♦ ♦

Bob Kendrick sits at a conference table at the Negro Leagues Baseball Museum offices, remembering details from that moment at FanFest during the 2001 All-Star Game. As he finishes that story, another "classic" Buck O'Neil moment pops into his mind.

The two, along with Don Motley, the Executive Director of the Negro Leagues Baseball Museum, were at a Kansas State football game, guests of school President Jon Wefald. The trip to Manhattan, Kansas, to watch the Wildcats and visit Wefald, their friend and a supporter of the NLBM, was a tradition for Kendrick and O'Neil.

As usual, this one particular year — the exact year and opponent are fuzzy to Kendrick right now — the President's suite was full as people spoke quietly while watching the action on the field. Out of the blue, after an inconsequential play transpired, O'Neil jumped up and shouted: "Go Jayhawks!"

"The room just erupted in laughter," Kendrick says. "That was Buck."

Besides a quick wit, Buck O'Neil had an infectious personality. When he walked into a room, people gravitated toward him. As Kendrick says, "Buck never met a stranger in his life." At the same time, he had a unique ability to make each person feel as if he or she were the only person in the room.

"He genuinely loved people," Kendrick added. "He had great respect for humanity. That, I think, is probably the greatest thing I've learned and I hope some of that rubbed off on me. Few of us can bridge the gap between black and white, young and old, men and women, but Buck did.

"That compassion is one of the hallmarks that I certainly relate to Buck. The man was charming and witty and had all those great character traits that you admire."

The funny thing is that, regardless of his popularity and people clamoring for his attention, Buck never saw himself as a celebrity. He would always shrug off the notion. There wasn't an egotistical bone in his body.

"Traveling with him was absolutely crazy," said Kendrick. "So many people wanted his autograph and to have pictures taken with him that they would follow us out to our car or wherever we were headed. He was like a rock star. It also was very heart-warming to see him get that kind of respect and admiration from people who didn't even know him. Even when they didn't know he was Buck O'Neil, they'd give him that look like they knew he was *somebody*."

Then there was the Buck O'Neil that only a few people saw. The O'Neil away from the spotlight and all the fans. Although his character didn't change in private, O'Neil displayed a different side in those quiet moments.

"It showed how much of a deep-thinking individual he was," Kendrick says. "He'd sit and talk politics and sports and religion and all these kinds of things that he (was) rarely asked about. He loved to watch basketball games and talk about other sports.

"It was an enlightening opportunity for me, both professionally and personally, to have had the opportunity to have this man in my life. For that, I will be eternally grateful."

As will anyone who ever came in contact with John Jordan "Buck" O'Neil — the man who not only offered wonderful baseball stories from an era otherwise forgotten, but also showed us through his words and his actions that each person, regardless of race, sex or age is the same in God's eyes.

Maybe nothing illustrated that better than that little song O'Neil would coax groups into singing anytime he spoke. So, in honor of Buck, stand up, hold hands with someone nearby, and sing after him:

The greatest thing in all my life is loving you,
The greatest thing in all my life is loving you,
The greatest thing in all my life is loving you,
The greatest thing in all my life is loving you.

John Jordan "Buck" O'Neil
1911 - 2006

Courtesy of Gregg Riess Photography

Chapter 4

The Birth of the Negro Leagues

Not many people in the history of baseball had the type of career that pioneer Andrew "Rube" Foster had. When it came to baseball, Foster was ahead of his time in everything. He was a great hitter and pitcher — using a wicked screwball — a remarkable manager, and later a winning owner.

According to the Baseball Hall of Fame, Foster won 44 straight games in 1902 with the Cuban Giants. Although unsubstantiated — stats weren't kept closely then — it's been said that in the early 1900s, Foster won 51 games ... in one season. And, they say, he got the nickname "Rube" when he outpitched the great George "Rube" Waddell and the Philadelphia Athletics around 1904 or '05.

Foster was so effective that major-league manager John McGraw, in the early 1900s, asked Foster to help his New York Giants pitchers. The result was Christy Mathewson learned his "fadeaway" pitch from Foster. Largely because of that pitch, Mathewson went on to have a Hall-of-Fame career.

Foster became a player-manager for the Leland Giants in 1907, leading the team to a 110-10 record. He did so by employing a style

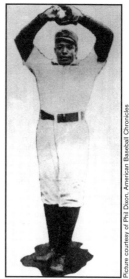

Picture courtesy of Phil Dixon, American Baseball Chronicles

Andrew "Rube" Foster. This photograph originally appeared in a July 1, 1905 edition of the *Philadelphia Evening Item*.

59

of baseball not seen anywhere else — using tactics such as the hit-and-run, bunt-and-run and aggressive base running.

His brother Willie, a great player in his own right, said: "Rube would start his man from first, and have his man that was hitting lay the ball down the third-base line. Since you were already stealing you (were expected to) make it to third."

Partnering with John C. Schorling, the brother-in-law of Chicago White Sox owner Charles Comiskey, Foster bought the Leland Giants a couple years later and changed their name to the Chicago American Giants. They became one of the most dominant black teams in baseball.

Based on Foster's track record, it stands to reason if someone would do it — form a unified black professional baseball league with the hopes of one day breaking Major League Baseball's color barrier, while providing an economic stimulus for African-Americans —Andrew "Rube" Foster would seem to be the most logical choice.

Indeed, Foster's greatest contribution to baseball stemmed from a meeting in 1920 at Kansas City's Paseo YMCA. To this day, it's unknown why the group met in Kansas City. In fact, according to reports in early 1920 in the *Indianapolis Freeman*, a black newspaper, the meeting was supposed to be held at the Freeman's offices in February 1920.

Kansas City's Paseo YMCA, 1930's

Regardless, on February 13 and 14, Foster brought together five other owners — C.I. Taylor of the Indianapolis ABC's, Joe Green of the Chicago Giants, J.L. Wilkinson of the Kansas City Monarchs, Lorenzo Cobb of the St. Louis Giants and J.T. Blount of the Detroit Stars — plus newspaper people Elwood C. Knox of the *Freeman*, Dave Wyatt and A.D. Williams of the *Indianapolis Ledger*, and Cary B. Lewis of the *Chicago Defender*, and they united to form the Negro National League.

There hadn't always been a need for a league specifically for African-American players. During the 1880s, several African-American players played in professional baseball leagues. The most notable is Moses "Fleet" Walker, who is regarded as the first African American to break the color barrier, in 1883, playing for Toledo of the American Association.

"Fleet" Walker's brother, Weldy, joined the club in 1884. Also of note, Bud Fowler played second base for Topeka, Kansas' Western League team. George Stovey played for teams in the Eastern League. Frank Grant was in that league, also. When Grant's team went out of business, he went to Buffalo of the International Association.

Meanwhile, however, prejudice was rearing its dastardly head. In 1883, the greatest white professional player of the day, "Cap" Anson of the Chicago White Stockings, announced he wouldn't play in an exhibition game against Toledo because of "Fleet" Walker. Anson changed his tune when he realized he'd lose his share of the gate receipts from that day's game. In 1887, Anson again balked at playing when the White Stockings were scheduled to play Stovey's Newark Little Giants in an exhibition. Stovey didn't play. Anson did.

Sol White, a former Negro leagues player, manager and historian, wrote in his book *History of Colored Base Ball* that the New York Giants wanted to buy Stovey's contract from Newark: "This same Anson ... made strenuous and fruitful opposition to any proposition looking to the admittance of a colored man in the National League."

Anson was just part of the trend. Two months after the game in which Stovey didn't play, several members of the St. Louis Browns of the American Association refused to play in a game against the Cuban Giants, an all-black team. Teams throughout pro baseball stopped signing African Americans. And, players such as the Walker brothers, Fowler, Stovey and Grant weren't re-signed by their predominantly white teams.

Unfortunately, between the late 1800s and the meeting at the Paseo YMCA in 1920, black baseball wasn't organized. Local all-black teams would play either against one another, against all-white teams or occasionally against groups of big leaguers barnstorming during the off-season. And, it was common before 1920 for players to jump from team to team during the season. Many deemed black baseball to be semi-pro, not because of the ability of the players, but because of the sand that formed the teams' foundation.

"Rube" Foster

Courtesy of the NLBM

61

The Negro National League, as Foster saw it, would validate black baseball and provide an economic stimulus by allowing only African-Americans to own and run teams. Each owner in attendance paid $500 to join the league. The newspaper men, along with Topeka attorney Elisha Scott, worked through the night to form the league's rules and write the constitution. The next day, February 14, the owners signed off on the constitution for the National Association of Colored Professional Base Ball Clubs, and became charter members of the Negro National League.

◆ ◆ ◆

James Leslie Wilkinson

The only exception to Rube Foster's rule of black ownership was James Leslie Wilkinson, a white businessman and baseball aficionado. Wilkinson, who founded the multi-racial All-Nations baseball team, came to Kansas City with that barnstorming club in 1915. Foster searched for a black owner for Kansas City before the meeting in 1920, but realized Wilkinson was fair to his players and would do what was best for them.

Wilkinson, who was known as "Wilkie," took some of the best players from his All-Nations team and some from the 25th Infantry Wreckers, an all-black U.S. Army team, and started to build the Kansas City Monarchs. He ended up assembling one of the best organizations in the history of the Negro Leagues.

The Monarchs, who became known as black baseball's version of the New York Yankees, won 10 Negro League pennants, tying the Homestead Grays for the most in Negro Leagues history. They also won the Negro World Series in 1924 and '42.

Of course, in order to be as successful, they needed quality players. They had great ones. Guys such as James "Cool Papa" Bell, Turkey Stearnes, Newt Allen, Satchel Paige, Ernie Banks and, of course, Buck O'Neil, all played for the Monarchs at some point during their careers.

Satchel Paige, Hall of Fame Pitcher

TOP 10 MONARCHS

The following list, provided by the Negro Leagues Baseball Museum, was formed by J.L. Wilkinson, the original Monarchs owner, and Tom Baird, who bought the team from Wilkinson in 1948. The all-time Monarchs list, which includes three pitchers (hence, 11), came from a 1950 publication called *Your Kansas City and Mine*. The names are in order by position.

11. *John Donaldson,* Pitcher
10. *Wilber "Bullet" Rogan,* Pitcher
 9. *Leroy "Satchel" Paige,* Pitcher
 8. *Frank Duncan,* Catcher
 7. *John "Buck" O'Neil,* First Base
 6. *Newton Allen,* Second Base
 5. *Walter "Doby" Moore,* Shortstop
 4. *Walter Lee "Newt" Joseph,* Third Base
 3. *Cristobal Torriente,* Right Field
 2. *Hurley Allen McNair,* Center Field
 1. *Oscar "Heavy" Johnson,* Left Field

In 1931, two years after the start of the Great Depression, most of the Negro National League teams also fell on hard times. Because of Wilkinson's passion for baseball and the popularity of the club, the Monarchs were one of the few teams that survived the Depression. Instead of staying home, hoping the fans would show up, Wilkinson turned the Monarchs into a barnstorming club. They traveled throughout the Midwest, complete with grandstands and *lights*.

You know the stories you've heard about how the Cincinnati Reds introduced the world to night baseball in 1935? That's not exactly true. Actually, J.L. Wilkinson and the Monarchs first played night baseball five years earlier. He invested his own money in a portable lighting system and the Monarchs became the first professional team to play under the lights.

With the Monarchs, one of the biggest draws, gone from the league and the Depression setting in, the NNL didn't make it. Another version of the NNL began in 1933 and lasted through the '48 season. Many of those teams joined the Negro American League, which was formed in 1937. The Monarchs were one of the nine original teams in the NAL.

Wilkinson did one more thing that changed baseball forever: he signed Jackie Robinson to his first pro baseball contract in 1945. Robinson spent one season with the Monarchs before he signed with the Brooklyn Dodgers and broke baseball's color barrier in 1947. That same season, three more African-American players reached the major leagues: Larry Doby for Cleveland, along with former Monarchs Hank Thompson and Willard Brown, both with the St. Louis Browns.

Ironically, the main goal for the Negro leagues, to integrate Major League Baseball, was the very thing that started the league's demise.

The year after Robinson broke in with the Dodgers, realizing the imminent fate of the Negro leagues, Wilkinson sold the Monarchs to Tom Baird. In 1955, the first year that the major league's A's planted roots in Kansas City, Baird sold the Monarchs to Ted Rasberry. They continued playing, mainly as a barnstorming team, until the early 1960s.

Jackie Robinson, as Brooklyn Dodgers second baseman, steals home plate.

"Wilkie" Wilkinson, who died in 1964 in a Kansas City nursing home at the age of 90, was inducted into the Baseball Hall of Fame in 2006.

◆ ◆ ◆

Andrew "Rube" Foster never got close to seeing his dream of black baseball players — particularly an entire team from the Negro National League — reach the Major Leagues. In 1926, showing early signs of a mental illness and exhaustion from trying to mold the Negro National League, Foster was admitted to the Illinois State Hospital in Kankakee. He died there in December 1930, about the same time as his Negro National League faded.

"To give you some idea of what Rube Foster meant to us," Buck O'Neil said, "people filed past his casket for three days after his funeral in Chicago, which was one of the largest funerals ever to take place there."

Although the Negro National League wasn't the same after the Depression in 1929, Rube Foster provided an early outlet that eventually changed the face of baseball. And, in the process, thanks to a meeting in 1920 at the Paseo YMCA, left Kansas City with a legacy that extends beyond the area.

1924 Kansas City Monarchs

Courtesy of the NLBM and Phil Dixon, American Baseball Chronicles

Chapter 5

A's Move West and Bring the "Majors" to Kansas City

It's hard to believe that this is actually the place. It looks so different now, just an open space with tall grass colored by dandelions. And it's quiet. No construction today of the homes that boast "Luxury Living in the City" — or at least that's what the sign promises. But, there's a light pole, about where second base used to be. There's a new house over there, around left field.

There's Lincoln High School a couple hundred yards away, where Royals Hall of Famer Frank White used to stand atop the football field's bleachers with his friends to catch a glimpse of what was happening on the other side of the fence. White's childhood home is just a few blocks away. As is the 18th and Vine District. And the aroma of Arthur Bryant's has made its way up here.

Indeed, this is the spot, 22nd and Brooklyn, the site of the old Municipal Stadium. This is where it all began for Major League Baseball in Kansas City, in 1955, when the Philadelphia Athletics moved west and called this place home.

"That was a long time ago," says Art Ditmar, who came up with the

Kansas City Municipal Stadium at 22nd & Brooklyn

Courtesy of Jim Chappell

Philadelphia A's in 1954 and then stayed with the club during its first two seasons in Kansas City.

Yep, in April 1955, Kansas City joined the ranks of Major League Baseball, thanks largely to a poor team in Philly and a Chicago businessman named Arnold Johnson, who didn't intend to become a Major League owner.

Several years before moving the A's, Johnson's entry into Major League Baseball and Kansas City was an afterthought. He originally wanted to purchase Yankee Stadium from his friends, Del Webb and Dan Topping. But the two men insisted that Johnson also buy their Class AAA stadium, Blues Stadium, in Kansas City. Johnson acquiesced and, unwittingly, moved Kansas City toward becoming a major-league city.

In his book, *The Kansas City Athletics*, former *Kansas City Star* sports editor Ernie Mehl wrote that even though Johnson didn't want to stand in the way of Kansas City getting a Major League team, Johnson didn't show an interest in owning one.

In fact, when asked if he wanted to own a Major League team, Johnson replied, "Not in the slightest."

After unsuccessful attempts by Connie Mack, his family and several Philadelphia businessmen to keep the Athletics from moving, in the winter of 1954, Johnson changed his tune and purchased the Athletics for a reported $3.5 million.

Kansas City finally was going to be a major-league city. Mehl added of the city's celebration upon hearing the news: "Nothing like it had been seen since the signing of the armistice of World War I."

The only major piece left in the move was changing Municipal Stadium from a minor-league park to one for a Major League team. Besides the Blues, the Municipal-Blues-Ruppert-Muehlbach Stadium, which originally was constructed in 1923 for $400,000, also had previously been home to the Monarchs of the Negro Leagues.

In essence, in 22 weeks, the stadium was rebuilt. A second deck was added and Johnson purchased the old Braves Field scoreboard in Boston for $100,000 and put it in right-center field.

During that 1955 season, the Kansas City Athletics drew a whopping 1,393,054 fans, a far cry from the 304,666 in their final season in Philadelphia. The attendance in '55 was the largest ever in the history of Municipal, including the Royals' four seasons there.

"Our desire to go to the ballpark wasn't as strong in Philadelphia as it was in Kansas City," said Ditmar, who led the club in wins in 1955 and '56, with 12 each season. "The new Municipal was great, but it was greater having people in the stands."

The players received a heroes' welcome for opening day in 1955. There was a grand parade in downtown Kansas City, with an estimated 200,000 people crowding the streets.

"I will never forget that parade," Ditmar says. "They held a huge blowout for us unlike anything else I had seen."

New home or not, though, to the Athletics' opponents, the change of cities didn't make a big difference. It still was the team that went 51-103 in '54.

"Sure, we felt confident that we could beat them," said Kansas City area resident Hank Bauer, who was a key player for the Yankees during 1948-59 before finishing his career with the Kansas City A's in 1961.

For the 1955 A's, it was a brand new experience. They responded by beating Detroit on opening day. They won 62 more times that season, while losing 91. The team finished sixth in the American League (out of eight teams). Still, players such as Ditmar labeled it a "good year."

Courtesy of Jim Chappell

The 1961 Kansas City A's

Sitting: Ron Turley and Mike Woods, Batboys. **Front Row, left to right:** Bill Kunkel, Ted Wilks, Dario Lodigiani, Joe Gordon, Joyner White, Ed Fitzgerald, Dick Howser, Wayne Causey, Al Pilarcik, Jay Hankins, Bud Daley, Ray Herbert. **Second Row, left to right:** Dave Keefe, Traveling Secretary, Lou Klimchock, Jerry Walker, Dave Wickersham, Ed Keegan, Ken Johnson, Norm Bass, Joe Nuxhall, Norm Siebern, Don Larsen, Haywood Sullivan, Clay Reid, Equipment Manager. **Back Row, left to right:** Bill Jones, Trainer, Andy Carey, Leo Posada, Ed Rakow, Jerry Lumpe, Hank Bauer, Jim Archer, Bill Tuttle, Joe Pignatano, Bob Boyd, Chuck Essigian, Marv Throneberry

There weren't many good years during the Athletics' existence in Kansas City. They never finished above .500, and they lost 90 games or more in nine of their 13 seasons.

Still, there were some memorable moments and characters, led by the eventual top man, Charles O. Finley, who bought 51 percent of the club in December 1960. An insurance broker by trade, Finley was a true hands-on owner.

His best-known antics included a mule as the team mascot, a mechanical rabbit that brought baseballs to the home-plate umpire, sheep in right field and a petting zoo.

"I liked to hit fungos to our right fielder before the game, and hit them as far as I could to see if I could hit some sheep," joked former pitcher Moe Drabowsky in 2005, about a year before losing a battle with cancer.

"I felt sorry for the shepherd who had to tend to the sheep. He wore a toga and his head was wrapped up. Imagine how hot that was. He used to get something like $10 per game to tend to those sheep. On doubleheaders he thought he should've gotten $20, and he told Charley that. During the next doubleheader, I noticed that he wasn't there. We never saw the shepherd again. I guess Charley didn't think he deserved $20."

Drabowsky, who was the opening day starter in 1965, was another of the memorable characters. Two weeks after that initial start, the A's shipped Drabowsky to Class AAA Vancouver. Thinking his career was over, he almost balked at going.

"Until I looked at the schedule and saw that they played twice in Hawaii," he said. "I'd never been to Hawaii, so I took the assignment to Vancouver. I didn't pitch that well, but I enjoyed Hawaii immensely."

Some of the other players who played for the A's in Kansas City

include Norm Siebern, Charley Lau, Lew Krausse, Reggie Jackson, Satchel Paige (at age 59ish) and Bert Campaneris. In fact, on September 8, 1965, Campaneris played all nine positions in one game. (Of course, that was right around the time that the A's drew

Lew Krausse, Jr., the Kansas City A's $125,000 bonus pitcher, June 16, 1961.

an all-time low of 690 fans during one afternoon game.)

While in Kansas City, the club's roster also included hometown products Don Buschhorn, Chuck Dobson, Alex George, Paul Lindblad and John O'Donoghue.

Following the 1967 season, after a failed attempt to move the team to Dallas five years earlier, Finley closed shop at Municipal and moved the Athletics to Oakland.

"We were glad to move. It was so poor here that crowds dwindled to nothing," said Dobson. "We had big dreams of going to California, seeing how the (Los Angeles) Dodgers and the (San Francisco) Giants were doing well. There were 50,000 people at our opening day. The next day there were 5,000. We drew terribly out there until we started winning.

"Plus, Kansas City deserved better than Charley Finley's A's."

Funny, but the best thing Finley might've done in Kansas City (besides leaving, some would contend) happened away from baseball. Finley paid the Beatles a then-record $150,000 to perform for 30 minutes at Municipal Stadium on September 17, 1964.

Even though the A's were pitiful on the field during their time in Kansas City, at least one thing remained constant: Municipal Stadium.

"The first thing that comes to mind is the ballpark and (former groundskeeper) George Toma," said current St. Louis Cardinals manager Tony LaRussa, who played for the A's in 1963. "I had never seen a field so beautiful in all my life. The pride and the craftsmanship that he and his crew displayed were incredible.

"I was so young and overwhelmed that besides our club being overmatched and playing where we didn't belong, I don't remember much else."

Two years after the A's bolted, in 1967, the anti-Finley, Ewing Kauffman, bought the expansion Royals. They occupied the same Municipal Stadium for four years, and quickly won over the hearts of the forlorn Kansas City fans.

"Since the A's left Kansas City high and dry, fans really wanted the Royals to crush the A's," Royals broadcaster Denny Matthews, who's been with the club since its inception, wrote in his book, *Tales from the Royals Dugout*. "We haven't seen that intense distaste since."

Drabowsky, who earned the distinction in 1969 of becoming a player to play for both the Kansas City A's and the Royals, picked up the first win in Royals' history, when Kansas City beat Minnesota

4-3 in 12 innings on opening day. (In that game, another former K.C. A's pitcher, Dave Wickersham, got the save.)

"It was such a delight to get that win," said Drabowsky, who ended the 1969 season with 11 wins and 11 saves. "Joining the club with some younger kids, they needed some veterans, and thought I could help. I certainly loved coming back."

Despite the rivalry between the two clubs that have called Kansas City home, players for the Athletics point out, win or lose, the fans that did show up supported the club.

"It was a great relationship between the fans and the players," said Ditmar. "1955 and '56 were as good as any two years I had in baseball, including World Series appearances."

"I like Kansas City, which is why I stayed here," said Bauer, who also played for the Blues when they were a Yankees' farm club. "I thought the fans in Kansas City were outstanding. It wasn't like New York; Kansas City fans didn't boo too many people."

TOP 10 A's

10. Bob Cerv, Outfield, 1957-60
9. Harry "Suitcase" Simpson, Outfield/First Base, 1955-57
8. Dick Howser, Infield, 1961-63
7. Dick Green, Infield, 1963-67
6. Vic Power (who also played for the Blues), Infield, 1955-58
5. Rocky Colavito, Outfield, 1964
4. Jim Gentile, Infield, 1964-65
3. Bert Campaneris, Infield, 1964-67
2. Roger Maris, Outfield, 1958-59
1. Jim "Catfish" Hunter, Pitcher, 1965-67

Author's Note: Long-time Kansas City Star *sportswriter Sid Bordman, who covered the Blues, A's and Royals for the paper, compiled most of this list. Although the task is impossible, especially considering there were some bad A's teams in Kansas City, Bordman's first nine picks and my final one, should give you an idea of some of the players who played in Kansas City.*

TOP 10 BLUES

Although Kansas City had its first professional baseball team in 1884 in the form of the Union Association's Cowboys, the first local team to use the name Blues started in 1888. The Blues club with which long-time fans are familiar was one of the original members of the American Association in 1902. With the A's coming to Kansas City from Philadelphia, the Blues' final game was on September 12, 1954, before they moved to Denver. During their half-century here, though, the Blues finished first in the AA in 1918, '23, '29, '39, '40, '42 and '47. They won the AA pennant in 1918, '23, '29, '38, '52 and '53. They won the Little World Series in '23 and '29, and the Junior World Series in '38, two years after becoming a farm team for the New York Yankees.

10. Bob Cerv
9. Elston Howard
8. Al Rosen
7. Bunny Brief
6. Bill Skowron
5. Joe Cronin
4. Mickey Mantle
3. Whitey Ford
2. Hank Bauer
1. Phil Rizzuto

Author's Note: Long-time Kansas City Star *sportswriter Sid Bordman, who was a batboy and then an assistant trainer with the Blues before covering the Blues, A's and Royals with* The Star, *compiled most of this list. (During his time with the Blues, incidentally, he roomed with future Hall of Famer Yogi Berra in spring training in Excelsior Springs.) Although the task is impossible, considering the Blues' time in Kansas City, Bordman's first seven picks and my final three should give you an idea of some of the players who played in Kansas City.*

"Where Have You Gone?"

HANK BAUER

Hank Bauer taps his hands on the round tabletop as he thinks about the question for several seconds.

"What am I most proud of or what do I want to be remembered for more?" he repeats in a gravelly voice — partially the result of surgery for throat cancer — while glancing at the television on the "veranda" of his Lenexa home to see how Tiger Woods is doing at the 2006 American Express Championship.

"I'm most proud of my time in the Marines, but I'm remembered more for my time with the Yankees."

That's probably the best way for Bauer, who sports a crew cut, to answer the question. After all, he's lived a hero's life, times two.

In baseball, he played 14 years in the major leagues, most notably as a right fielder with the New York Yankees, during which time he went to nine World Series, coming away with seven championship rings. He spent his last two seasons, 1960-61, with the Kansas City A's, including his last as a player-manager.

As impressive as his time in baseball, though, there's Hank Bauer the Marine. In 1942, he signed up for Jimmy Roosevelt's 4th Raider Battalion, which was responsible for making beachheads for more Marines and the Army. They made four landings.

The Battalion's fourth and final landing started on Easter Sunday, 1945, on Okinawa. During the 53rd day of fighting, Bauer was shot in the left leg. The platoon started with 64 men. Six survived.

Bauer, who was wounded by shrapnel at Guam and had 23 bouts of malaria, earned two Purple Hearts and a Bronze Star for his heroism.

"I don't know why I volunteered; I guess I was gung-ho," said Bauer, who got out in 1946 with the rank of Platoon Sergeant. "I don't volunteer for anything anymore."

Bauer, who has called Kansas City home since 1947, played for the Kansas City Blues, a Yankees farm team, for two years before the Yankees called him up in September 1948. For the next 11-plus seasons, he played in right, alongside centerfielders Joe DiMaggio and Mickey Mantle.

When it comes to choosing the better player between the two, Bauer takes the high road and picks "DiMaggio in his day and Mickey in his day." But, DiMaggio helped make Bauer's first game at Yankee Stadium memorable.

The second batter of the game hit a fly ball to right-center. Bauer ran over, called for it and caught it. For some reason, though, DiMaggio kept staring at Bauer after the play.

Bauer said: "After the inning, we were down in the runway and I said, 'Joe, did I do something wrong out there? You kept looking at me.' He said, 'No, you didn't do anything wrong, but you're the first son of a (gun) that invaded my territory.' I didn't do it anymore after that."

A dependable player during the regular season, Bauer excelled during the World Series. Besides a long-time record 17-game hitting streak in the Series, Bauer came up especially big in 1951 and '58.

During the sixth and final game against the New York Giants in '51, Bauer hit a bases-loaded triple in the sixth inning, which put the Yankees up 4-3. He also made a run-scoring sliding catch that ended the game. Then, in 1958, against the Milwaukee Braves, Bauer hit four homers.

As if seven world championships as a player weren't enough, including five in a row from 1949-53, Bauer led the Baltimore Orioles to a four-game sweep over the Los Angeles Dodgers in the 1966 Series as manager.

"It's a lot easier playing in the World Series than managing in one," he quips.

These days, Bauer doesn't go to Kauffman Stadium much anymore. He makes it to Yankee Stadium each year for Old-Timers' Day, but he prefers watching the Royals and his beloved Yankees on TV with the "Extra Innings" package.

"If I don't like what's happening with the Royals or Yankees, I'll flick it," said Bauer, whose wife of nearly 50 years, Charlene, a former secretary with the Kansas City Blues, passed away in 1998. "I can watch six to 10 games a night, but I flick a lot."

Even though he's recognized in public and continues to receive six to eight autograph requests in the mail each day, Bauer doesn't dwell on his career. The only baseball reminders around his home are a painting of himself in the living room and his 1953 World Series ring.

"I don't ever think about (my career)," he said. "I'm just thankful that I was blessed to play with so many great players. Some guys play their entire careers without ever going to a World Series. It was a great honor for me to play."

**Enos Slaughter's Kansas City Athletics bat
signed by the 1955 Athletics.**

Courtesy of Gregg Riess Photography

Chapter 6

The City Gets a Fresh Start with Royals

Sportswriters are often a challenge for owners. But seldom more than these two from Kansas City, in 1967. Oh, sure, many sportswriters throughout the years have believed — true or not — that they have impacted sports. They have the ability to point out obvious shortcomings about someone in the front office or a manager or a coach on the field, providing some additional fire power (pun intended). Or the ability to praise a slumping player and get the fans behind him.

There have been few sportswriters, though, who have made such a huge impact on a city as Ernie Mehl and Joe McGuff, long-time scribes and editors for *The Kansas City Star*.

As McGuff pointed out in a column that ran in *The Star* in September 1995, it was Mehl who made the biggest crusade, back in 1953, to turn Kansas City into a major-league sports town to help give the area a post-World War II economic boost.

"His push against a wall of indifference reignited the spirit of a city already famous for jazz, soon to be noted for barbecue and sports, and now poised for a cultural renaissance with an upcoming downtown entertainment district, performance arts center and expanded art gallery," wrote McGuff, who served on the Royals Board of Directors from 1994 to 2000.

Mehl's persistency paid off when Arnold Johnson, a Chicago businessman, bought the Philadelphia A's and moved them to Kansas City in '55.

In spite of the A's performance during their 13 seasons in Kansas City and the foul taste that owner Charlie Finley left with many in the area, Mehl and McGuff started pleading with major-league owners to bring baseball back to Kansas City before the owners approved Finley's move to Oakland. Mehl and McGuff enlisted the help of several local business leaders and U.S. Senator Stuart Symington from, ironically, St. Louis.

After the 1967 season, when the owners approved Finley's move, they guaranteed the Kansas City delegation that baseball would be back in the city before 1971. By at least one account, the owners simply said when it was "practical," not actually giving a date. Either way, that wasn't good enough. Too many things could go wrong — i.e. the owners changing their minds — in those four years. That's when Sen. Symington stepped in.

"He told (the owners) that wasn't acceptable," said McGuff, "and when he went back to Washington, he would work to rectify this, the implication being that he would try to change their anti-trust exemption."

By the end of those meetings, Kansas City was guaranteed an expansion franchise for 1969, along with Seattle (the Pilots, who moved shortly thereafter to Milwaukee and became the Brewers), Montreal and San Diego.

The elated local group began a search for someone to buy the club. They found it in a somewhat unlikely person when long-time Kansas Citian and pharmaceutical millionaire Ewing Kauffman, who wasn't a baseball fan and didn't know a lot about the game, stepped up to the plate for the city.

"(Businessmen) like Earl Smith and Les Milgram really got the thing rolling, and then Ewing's wife Muriel put him over the edge," said broadcaster Denny Matthews, who is one of a handful of people who has been with the club since its first season. "Muriel was the last one to kick him in the seat of the pants and say, let's do it."

Even though Kauffman didn't know much about baseball, he cared about two things: guarding his investment and winning. Charlie Metro, who started with the Royals in 1968 as the Director of Player Procurement and managed the club for 52 games in 1970, learned that firsthand during his initial interview with Kauffman. After hearing about the Royals, Metro asked Kauffman if he was more interested in making money or winning.

When Kauffman answered "both," Metro replied: "If you make money and we lose, are you going to be happy?"

Mr. and Mrs. Ewing Kauffman

Courtesy of the Kansas City Royals

"Heck, no," Kauffman replied. Being a wise, competitive businessman, Kauffman hired baseball people to run the organization. Possibly the best in the bunch was Cedric Tallis, who had been the California Angels' vice-president in charge of operations. Kauffman first met Tallis during a trip to California when Kauffman was considering purchasing the Royals.

Kauffman hired Tallis as the Royals Executive Vice-President/General Manager on January 16, 1968. Tallis quickly assembled a staff that included Lou Gorman, Joe Burke, Herk Robinson and John Schuerholz.

"I'm not so sure anyone knew what an excellent franchise they were creating," said Schuerholz, who admitted that he had to think twice about leaving the Baltimore organization, where he had spent two years with Lou Gorman, because he pictured Kansas City as "cowboy hats and horses attached to hitching posts in front of the general store."

"The organization was consistently dedicated and focused on doing things as best as they could be done in the baseball industry. Mr. K gets most of the credit for (the franchise's success) because he set such high standards," according to Scheuerholz.

Besides the great front-office personnel hirings, Tallis' abilities as General Manager appeared quickly on the field, too. Before the 1969 season, through trades, Tallis acquired key players such as catcher Buck Martinez and '69 Rookie of the Year Lou Piniella. After that first season, when the Royals won 69 games, Tallis sent Joe Foy to the New York Mets for future Royals star Amos Otis and Bob Johnson. Then in two other deals before 1971, Tallis also acquired future team Hall of Famers Cookie Rojas and Fred Patek (in a six-player deal that sent Johnson to the Pirates).

"I went from the World Champion Mets, as a third baseman and outfielder, to an expansion team," said Otis, who was in the Royals first Hall of Fame class in 1986. "It turned out to be the best move in my career because I became an everyday centerfielder, which is what I wanted to do."

Courtesy of the Kansas City Royals

The Kansas City Royals, 1969

In addition to Otis, Patek and Rojas, Tallis' trades brought other Royals Hall of Fame players John Mayberry and Hal McRae.

Kauffman also gave Tallis major responsibilities in the development and construction of Royals Stadium, which became the Royals' home in 1973 after their first four seasons in Municipal Stadium. (As Kauffman learned when they first met, Tallis had been instrumental in the building of Anaheim's stadium.) That's the way it was with Kauffman and his "associates" as he called them. He stayed back and let them run the organization.

"He was hands off, but his aura was always around us," Schuerholz said. "We knew we couldn't disappoint Mr. K. We knew what he expected and the confidence he had in us."

Through a combination of the right people in the front office and on the field, the Royals developed into a championship-caliber team in a relatively short amount of time.

The club's tenure in Kansas City has produced many more highlights and great players, with fewer peculiarities and greater fan support than its predecessor Athletics. Maybe it was fitting that the Royals captured their first American League West title in 1976 by beating, of all teams, the Oakland A's.

"When you're in the pennant race every year," Otis said, "even if you're not in a big city, you feel like you're in one. We were treated great off the field and we played in full stadiums. When other teams came to Kansas City, they knew they had their hands full."

That must be what the baseball owners realized in the fall of 1967.

Top 10 Kansas City Baseball Stadiums

Kansas Citians have enjoyed professional baseball for 140 years in approximately 14 local sites, including the two current facilities, Kauffman Stadium and CommunityAmerica Ballpark. The following is a list of 10 stadiums and/or fields in Kansas City's professional baseball history.

10. *Exercise Field* — 14th and McGee — Antelopes, 1866.

 9. *Athletic Park* — Southwest Blvd. and Summit — Union Association's Unions, 1884.

 8. *Pastime Park* — Southwest Blvd. and Broadway — Cowboys of the Western League, 1885.

 7. *League Park* — Independence and Lydia — Cowboys teams in three leagues, 1886-89.

 6. *Exposition Park* — 15th and Montgall — Blues teams in three leagues, 1888-1902.

 5. *Sportsman's Park* — 17th and Indiana — Blue Stockings of the Western League, 1902-03.

 4. *Shelly Park* — Independence and Oak — Royal Giants, 1910-15.

 3. *Association Park* — 19th and Olive — Class AA Blues, 1903-22; Monarchs, 1920-22.

 2. *Parade Park* — 17th and The Paseo —Kansas City Monarchs, 1930s and '40s.

 1. *Municipal Stadium* — 22nd and Brooklyn — Also called Muehlebach Stadium, Blues Stadium and Monarchs Stadium, it was home to four professional teams from 1923-72 (excluding 1968): Class AA Blues (1923-54), Monarchs (1923-54), Athletics (1955-67) and the Royals (1969-72). It also was the early home of the Kansas City Chiefs.

Source: "Unions to Royals"

Chapter 7

Royals Players
and Moments

Your first time is always memorable. Regardless of what you're doing.

Somehow, though, the 1980 Royals are often forgotten. Or at least just a side note. It's easy to understand the reason. Despite being the first Major League team from Kansas City to reach the World Series, the '80 club that lost to Philadelphia is often overshadowed by the team that won it all five years later.

In many ways, though, it's the 1980 team that serves as the link between the perennial playoff teams of the 1970s to the 1985 World Series championship.

"With the players who were here for an extended period of time, like Amos Otis, John Mayberry and Fred Patek, and because of the success we had then on the field, I think we identify with a different group of fans than the players in '85 and certainly the players of today," said Dennis Leonard, who pitched for the Royals during 1974-86, but missed the 1985 World Series because of a knee injury suffered two years earlier.

The 1980 season was full of firsts for the Royals. For guys such as George Brett, who flirted with ending the season with a .400 batting average, and Willie Wilson, who swatted a league-leading (and still Royals' record) 230 hits. And for a submarine pitcher named Dan Quisenberry, who burst onto the scene.

Another first awaited the Royals on the other side of the regular season, in which the club finished 97-65. Despite some classic series, the Yankees had defeated the Royals in the American League playoffs in 1976, '77 and '78. The most bitter was 1977 when, in the decisive fifth game, the Royals took a 3-2 lead into the top of the ninth at home but lost 5-3.

"We were really frustrated, especially in '77 because we thought we had the better team, but it didn't work out that way," said Leonard. "Sooner or later we knew it would work out. Sooner or later we were going to beat the Yankees."

Indeed, they would. Behind solid pitching along with great offense and defense by ALCS Most Valuable Player Frank White, the Royals took a quick two games to none lead over the Yankees.

During Game 3 in New York, the Royals led 1-0 in the top of the fifth inning on a homer by White. Then, trailing 2-1 in the top of the seventh, Brett came to the plate with two on and faced Yankees' flamethrower Rich "Goose" Gossage.

Proving that there was something magical about the 1980 season, Brett launched Gossage's first pitch into the stands in right. Brett has since called that the biggest hit of his career.

"Time flies, but I can remember all of it so vividly," Brett said 25 years later. "I remember rounding the bases and how quiet Yankee Stadium got. Usually when we were there it was the loudest place you'd ever been. To get a hit that silenced everybody was unbelievable."

The stadium started to roar again in the ninth inning. The Yankees

George Brett
Royals Third Baseman
1973-93

loaded the bases with no outs against Quisenberry. But as quick as — pardon the expression — a New York minute, shortstop U.L. Washington caught a line drive off the bat of Rick Cerone and doubled off Reggie Jackson at second base. Quiz caught the next batter, Willie Randolph, looking at a sinker down and in, ending the game. And the Royals' miseries.

"It's hard to describe how gratifying it was to beat the Yankees," said Leonard, who won Game 2. "I couldn't have dreamed of beating them in three games. All our other series proved differently, but I think the law of averages was on our side in 1980."

Said Brett: "It was a great thrill not only to beat the Yankees but to get the hit that beat them. Looking at my career, I'm most proud of that hit."

However, over the next few days, instead of coming back to Kansas City and relaxing or even reveling in the city's excitement, the Royals, knowing they were going to be traveling to the N.L. city, stayed in New York, awaiting the winner of the Philadelphia-Houston series.

"There was some confusion about what to do, and maybe if we came home and rested things might have been different," said Leonard. "Once you get on the field, though, you can't use it as an excuse."

In Game 1 against the Phillies, which Leonard started, Amos Otis put the Royals on top with a home run in the second inning. In doing so, Otis, who blistered the ball all Series, became just the 16th player to homer in his first World Series at-bat. He went on to lead the Royals at the plate with two more home runs and a .478 batting average.

"(Philadelphia) thought I was a fastball hitter, so they kept throwing me breaking balls," said Otis. "Pretty much every time up, I took the first pitch, which was usually a fastball, then they'd throw me a breaking ball and I'd hit it."

Not to be completely outdone, 1980 newcomer Willie Aikens hit at a .400 clip with four home runs in two games.

"I was fortunate to play with Amos until he retired, so I saw some of the things that he did in his career," said Leonard. "But (Otis and Aikens) both did an outstanding job. Everybody did. When you put the uniform on, especially on that stage, everybody's giving 100 percent. Sometimes it works out, sometimes it doesn't."

In the case of the 1980 Royals, it didn't. After tying the Series at two games apiece, the Phillies took the next two, clinching the championship.

Looking back now, more than 25 years later, it's easier for the players to have some additional fondness for that trip to the World Series.

"Playing in the World Series and producing the way I did was the highlight of my career," said Otis.

"I think about the standout players who go through their whole careers without a chance to go to the World Series," said Leonard. "Look at the Cubs with players like Ernie Banks and Billy Williams, to have the careers that they had and never play in the playoffs, let alone the World Series. Then to think that I was in the right place at the right time. It's really special."

Coincidentally, even though the 1980 Royals aren't remembered as easily as the '85 club, that first World Series moment was the impetus for what happened five years later.

"That experience (in 1980) whet our appetites about the World Series," said Brett. "The World Series wasn't beating the New York Yankees; it was beating someone from the other league. Sure enough we had that opportunity in 1985 and took advantage of it."

And gave Kansas City another first.

TOP 10 ROYALS PLAYERS

10t. *Mike Sweeney, Infielder, 1995-2006* *

Although he came up as a catcher, the Royals moved Mike Sweeney to first base in 1999. It was then that he started to emerge as the face of the Royals — the club's star player, the one his teammates have counted on to get a big hit when needed — as he batted .322 with 185 hits, 44 doubles, 22 home runs, 102 runs batted in and 101 runs scored. He followed that in 2000 with career-bests in hits (206), homers (29) and RBIs (144). Sweeney's fifth selection to the American League All-Star team in 2005 gave him the distinction of being one of four Royals all-time to be picked for the midsummer classic at least five times. (The others are George Brett, Amos Otis and Frank White.)

10t. *Carlos Beltran, Outfielder, 1998-2004*

The five-tool player — one who can hit for average, hit for power, has running speed, can play defense, and possesses a strong throwing arm — is a rarity in baseball. Amos Otis was the only five-tool player in Royals history until the switch-hitting Carlos Beltran came along. During his relatively short time with the Royals,

---

* Signed with Royals through 2007

Beltran, the AL Rookie of the Year in 1999, twice led the team in batting average, hits and home runs. On three occasions, he led the Royals in runs scored, triples and stolen bases. In 2002, Beltran played in all 162 games. He was part of the five-player trade in June 2004 that brought John Buck, Mark Teahen and Mike Wood to the Royals.

9. Dick Howser, Manager, 1981-87

It's funny how karma works in baseball. George Brett's famous homer off "Goose" Gossage in the 1980 ALCS not only gave the Royals their first trip to the World Series, but it also gave them the manager who would take them to their first World Championship.

In spite of winning a career-high 103 games in his first year as manager in '80, George Steinbrenner fired Dick Howser. About eight months later, during the 1981 baseball strike, when the Royals fired Jim Frey, Howser was broadcasting minor-league games on ESPN with long-time Royals announcer Fred White. Howser was the perfect fit for the Royals.

Howser, incidentally, was familiar with Kansas City before joining the Royals. He was selected as The Sporting News Rookie of the Year in 1961 while playing for the Kansas City A's. That year, he had career highs in average (.280), hits (171), doubles (29), triples (6), walks (92) and runs (108).

Although he's best known for leading the Royals to their World Series victory in 1985, Howser's best managing job may have come in 1984. Facing injuries throughout the season, the Royals sat in sixth place in the A.L. West on July 18 with a 40-51 record. During the final 10 weeks of the season, they went 44-27, and won the division. ESPN selected Howser as its Manager of the Year.

Three days after he managed the American League club in the 1986 All-Star Game, on July 18, doctors diagnosed Howser with a malignant brain tumor. Less than a year later, on June 17, 1987, Howser lost the battle. He was 51. That same year, his number 10 became the first number the Royals retired.

8. Dan Quisenberry, Pitcher, 1979-88

Dan Quisenberry and his submarine delivery emerged when the Royals desperately needed a closer in the bullpen..Sure, guys such as Al Hrabosky and Doug Bird had done the job previously, but not well enough to get past the Yankees in the postseason. In

Quiz's first full season as the club's closer, 1980, he led the Royals with a then-franchise-record 33 saves, which tied for the lead in the American League that year. He went on to lead the league in saves four more times, and was selected as the Royals Pitcher of the Year four times. He finished his career with 238 saves and a 2.55 earned run average.

"Quiz probably put fans in the best comfort zone of any pitcher the Royals have ever had," Fred White wrote in the book *Play by Play*. "No matter what the situation was, when he came into the ballgame, fans had the feeling that he was going to get out of any jam the team was in."

Quisenberry died from a brain tumor on September 30, 1998.

7. *Bret Saberhagen, Pitcher, 1984-91*

Coming off a drug scandal in 1983 and a pitching staff that was getting long in the tooth, the Royals made a bold statement in 1984 by going with a youth movement on the mound. The youngest of the bunch was Bret Saberhagen, who remains the youngest Royal to make his major-league debut, doing so on April 4, 1984, at the age of 19. The next season, en route to becoming the World Series MVP and the youngest pitcher in major-league history to win a Cy Young Award (as well as the first Royals pitcher to win the award), Saberhagen led the club in wins (20), complete games (10) and strikeouts (158). He is the last Royals pitcher to win at least 20 games, winning a franchise-record 23 in 1989 with a league-best 2.16 ERA. That year, he became the Royals only two-time Cy Young Award winner.

6. *Hal McRae, Designated Hitter/Outfielder, 1973-87*

Hal McRae is regarded as one of the best and most aggressive players ever to wear Royals' blue. His all-out play in the outfield and on the base paths as a designated hitter helped lead the Royals to five American League Championship Series and two World Series. In fact, because of McRae's aggressive play, especially after he practically knocked New York Yankees second baseman Willie Randolph into the outfield while breaking up a double play, Major League Baseball adopted the "McRae Rule." Best known as the club's DH, McRae, a lifetime .293 hitter, led the American League in RBIs in 1982 with 133. McRae went on to manage the Royals during 1991-94. One of his players during that time was his son Brian.

"McRae is one of the real pros of the game," said former general manager John Schuerholz. "As astute of a student of hitting as I have ever seen. And a clutch performer. When the game was on the line you wanted to have Brett or McRae at the plate."

5. Bo Jackson, Outfielder, 1986-90

He could do it all. During his brief time with the Royals, Bo Jackson hit the farthest home run at Kauffman Stadium, approximately 475 feet, on Sept. 14, 1986. (That was his first major-league homer, by the way.) A few years later, he led off the bottom of the first inning of the 1989 All-Star Game in Anaheim with a 448-foot shot. Defensively, he made one of the most memorable catches in Royals history at Baltimore's old Memorial Stadium in 1990, when he caught a ball at the warning track before running up the wall. Then, there was "the throw" (see "Top 10 Royals Moments" list). Not to mention, Bo was the first athlete to play in all-star games in both Major League Baseball and the NFL. Unfortunately for Royals fans, Jackson injured his hip in 1990 while playing football for the Los Angeles Raiders. The Royals released him during spring training in 1991.

4. Willie Wilson, Outfielder, 1976-90

For 15 seasons, Willie Wilson was a catalyst for the artificial-turf fast Royals clubs. He stole 668 bases, including a club-record 83 in 1979, was a two-time American League All-Star, won the A.L. batting title in 1982, and collected more than 100 hits from each side of the plate in 1980, helping lead the Royals to their first World Series appearance. In Game 7 of the 1985 Series against

Willie Wilson
Royals Outfielder, 1976-90

Courtesy of the Kansas City Royals

St. Louis, as the lead-off hitter, Wilson observed that starter John Tudor was in a pattern of throwing back-to-back fastballs and then a change-up to the Royals batters. Wilson relayed the information to his teammates, including Darryl Motley, who crushed Tudor's second-straight fastball, putting the Royals ahead for good in the Series-clinching game.

Courtesy of the Kansas City Royals

Amos Otis
Royals Outfielder
1970-83

3. *Amos Otis, Outfielder, 1970-83*

Acquired in a trade with the New York Mets before the 1970 season, Amos Otis was the Royals first great player. The team's first five-tool player. In 1970, he became the first Royal to play in the All-Star Game. Otis did it all, offensively and defensively. He routinely robbed hitters of home runs and extra-base hits. He went through a 165-game stretch during 1970-71 without an error. Offensively, he finished with 2,020 hits, 1,007 RBIs and 341 stolen bases. By the end of his 14-year career with the Royals, Otis was a three-time Royals Player of the Year winner, earned three Gold Glove awards and received five All-Star nominations. In 1986, he and Steve Busby were the first members of the Royals Hall of Fame.

2. *Frank White, Second Baseman, 1973-90*

Frank White is one of the greatest success stories in Royals history. After growing up in Kansas City and attending Lincoln High School, which didn't have a baseball team, White was working as a sheet-metal clerk when the Royals selected him from a tryout for their experimental Baseball Academy. The test paid off for the Royals. White played 18 seasons at second base in front of his hometown fans. During that time, he was an eight-time Gold Glove Award winner, a five-time All-Star, collected more than 2,000 hits, and, in 1985, became the second second baseman in major-league history to bat cleanup in the World Series. In 1980, he was the American League Championship Series MVP. His No. 20 was retired in 1995, nine years before the Royals honored him with a statue outside Kauffman Stadium.

1. *George Brett, Third Baseman, 1973-93*

The career numbers remain staggering: 3,154 hits, 317 home runs, 665 doubles, 137 triples, 201 stolen bases and three American League batting titles (the only person to earn one in three decades). Maybe it's appropriate, then, that many remember the player by a single number: 5. For 21 seasons, George Brett wowed Royals fans with his offensive numbers and his ability to come through in the clutch. The 1985 American League Championship Series MVP and eight-time Royals Player of the Year, Brett went on to become the first Royals player ever enshrined in the Baseball Hall of Fame, in 1999.

A LEGEND'S HIGH FIVE
FRANK WHITE

From Frank:

When you play as long as I did with as many talented players as we had, I have a lot of great memories. George's three batting titles, the "Pine Tar" game, Willie (Wilson) getting more than 100 hits from each side of the plate in 1980. It's hard to put them in a top 5 — I could easily come up with 20 things, but here you go:

1. Winning the 1985 World Series. That's why everyone plays, so that's definitely at the top for me. One thing that really stands out is Darryl Motley's home run in Game 7 after hitting one foul in almost the same spot. That really got us going in that final game.

2. Winning eight Gold Gloves, which meant I was the best at my position for so long. Along those lines, though, is not getting the ninth Gold Glove in 1988 when I committed just four throwing errors. I never counted on winning any awards when it came to a vote and I was always surprised when I won. But that was one time that I thought I'd get it and didn't. The cool thing was getting an award, a gold glove, from the fans after that happened.

3. Going to the 1980 World Series. We came so close the previous few years that it was rewarding to finally get there.

4. Batting fourth in all seven games of the 1985 World Series, and hitting the home run in Game 3 that helped us win our first World Series game ever. That was one of the longest home runs I ever hit.

5. The statue of me that the Royals erected at Kauffman Stadium in 2004. That was both a big surprise and a huge honor.

"Where Have You Gone?"

AMOS OTIS

"A.O., A.O., A.O. ..." the chant kept ringing. Normally, that particular echo for Amos Otis was reserved for Royals Stadium. This time, however, it was on the Royals' team bus.

The date was September 29, 1976. The first-place Royals were in the final game of a three-game set with the rival and second-place Oakland A's. Kansas City's lead in the standings had shrunk to 2½ games after dropping the first two matches in the series.

Otis, who had been beaned in the head two weeks earlier by Oakland pitcher Stan Bahnsen, was benched for those first two games.

Manager Whitey Herzog made sure Otis was in the lineup for the series finale. Along with an unlikely four-hitter by pitcher Larry Gura, Otis delivered an RBI double and a two-run home run as the Royals won 4-0. The win clinched at least a tie with the A's for the AL West title. The Royals went on to capture their first championship outright.

When Otis reached the team bus, the chant started.

"That's a very special feeling that's hard to describe," Otis said from his home in Henderson, Nev. "When you hear it from the fans it's wonderful, but when you hear it from your teammates, it's special. They chanted quite a while. It put me on top of the world. I appreciated it very much."

Otis, a mainstay in centerfield during 1970-83, did it all, offensively and defensively. He routinely robbed hitters of home runs and extra-base hits. He went through a 165-game stretch during 1970-71 without an error. (The superstitious Otis still contends that Royals broadcaster Denny Matthews broke the streak by mentioning it during a pre-game interview.) Offensively, Otis finished with 2,020 hits, 1,007 RBIs and 341 stolen bases.

"I worked on all phases of the game because I wanted to be a complete player," he said. "I didn't want to be a one-dimensional player."

An extra dimension to Otis' game wasn't well known until after he retired. He used a corked bat. Occasionally. Not often.

He quietly says it helped him hammer one of the most memorable home runs in Kauffman Stadium history, when the ball he hit off Rollie Fingers hit the flagpole in left field. Many people who saw it say that had the ball not hit the flagpole, it may have gone out of the stadium.

"I cranked it. There's an asterisk next to the person who hit the longest home run at Royals Stadium. People claim Bo Jackson got it, but I got it," Otis said, laughing. "Whenever I see Rollie Fingers he asks me if I had cork in my bat. I tell him it was loaded from top to bottom."

After his playing career ended in Pittsburgh in 1984, Otis coached briefly in the San Diego and Colorado organizations. Then, he walked away.

Since 1997, Otis has lived in the Las Vegas area with Beverly, his wife of 36 years. They travel to San Diego as much as possible to spend time with their grandchildren. Otis also finds a couple days a week to play golf.

"The more I play, the worse my game's getting, I think," said Otis, who was in Kansas City during the summer of 2006 for the "Legends" baseball game at CommunityAmerica Ballpark. "Baseball players are supposed to be good golfers. I can hit it far, but I can't always say where it's going. I had more control of where I hit a baseball than I do when I hit a golf ball."

To Royals fans, Otis' golf game doesn't matter. His baseball ability was good enough for fans to remember him. The fan mail he receives regularly is proof of that.

"Fan mail definitely gives me a good feeling because it means they haven't forgotten me," Otis said. "Sometimes people are writing for their kids, who probably never saw me, but as long as I'm being remembered, that's the best feeling."

Well, maybe that and having your teammates cheer for you.

TOP 10 ROYALS MOMENTS

10. *Quirk Calls His Shot*

It ranks as one of the most bizarre moments in Royals history. It wouldn't be so incredible to say that Jamie Quirk helped push the Royals into the playoffs. After all, Quirk was a dependable player during his three stints with the Royals: 1975-76, 1978-82 and 1985-88. Only, the time he helped the club the most, he was playing for the Cleveland Indians — and he told everyone he'd do it.

During the 1984 season, the Royals were in a pennant race with the Minnesota Twins. On September 24, the Indians acquired Quirk from the Chicago White Sox. Before reporting to the Indians, Quirk stopped in Kansas City to attend Paul Splittorff's retirement party. As the story goes, when Quirk left that night, he made a prediction.

"Yes, I jokingly made the comment that I would help beat the Twins and help (the Royals) into the playoffs," Quirk wrote in an e-mail interview for this book.

On Thursday the 27th, an off day, the Royals were headed to Oakland for the final series of the regular season. While at an airport, someone had a radio tuned to the Minnesota-Cleveland game. In the top of the ninth inning, Quirk went into the game as the Indians catcher. In the bottom of the inning, Quirk stepped up to the plate with two outs, nobody on base and the game tied at 3-3. Fred White, who was listening to the game with George Brett, one of Quirk's close friends, turned to Brett and said: "You don't suppose he's going to do that, do you?"

"Why else would he be there?" Brett replied. "Of course he's doing to do it."

And, he did. Quirk, facing Ron Davis, hit the longest home run of his career, into the upper deck at Cleveland's old Municipal Stadium.

"I was not thinking about the Royals as I was running the bases, but I was after the game," Quirk continued in the e-mail.

Quirk's game-winning home run, for all intents and purposes, knocked the Twins out of contention. The next day, the Royals clinched the division. That was Jamie Quirk's only at-bat with the Indians.

Quirk wrote: "It made for a great storyline."

9. Leo Beats "The Bird"

The 1976 Detroit Tigers featured rookie phenom pitcher Mark Fidrych, aka "The Bird." Before heading to Detroit for a series preceding the All-Star break, the Royals were in New York to play the Yankees. Royals manager Whitey Herzog told Dennis Leonard, a Brooklyn, N.Y., native, that he wasn't going to be pitching in New York because he made the All-Star team.

"Well, P.S.," Leonard says, "Whitey apologized to me later saying that he didn't know what happened, but I didn't make it. So, I went from being a big, tall stud, to become a little, itty-bitty nothing.

"My father-in-law, God bless him, flew to Detroit to meet us. We were in a little piano bar, I was drinking water, and I told him, 'Fidrych my [butt]. I'm going to beat him tomorrow.'"

In front of a capacity crowd at Tiger Stadium, Leonard and the Royals did just that, winning 1-0.

8. *Bo's Throw*

Certain things in life are easier to explain than "the throw": how toothpicks are made, why Elvis actually went into hiding in August 1977, reality TV. "The throw," however, can only be explained by saying the name Bo Jackson. There might not be another play or moment that better displayed Bo's baseball ability and super-human athleticism than his throw on June 5, 1989, in Seattle's Kingdome — the same place where Bo ran over Seahawks linebacker Brian Bosworth on Monday Night Football less than two years earlier. The unsuspecting Seattle athlete this time was Mariners second baseman Harold Reynolds.

The Royals and Mariners were tied 3-3 in the bottom of the 10th inning with Reynolds at first base, Scott Bradley and Steve Farr pitching for the Royals. Bradley lined the Farr offering into the left-field corner. The speedy Reynolds, who was running on the pitch, rounded third when Jackson grabbed the ball as it bounced off the wall. In a split instant, Jackson spun and, flat-footed with one foot on the warning track, fired a throw toward home plate. The throw, arguably one of the most accurate ever thrown by an outfielder, made it on the fly to catcher Bob Boone, an instant before Reynolds reached the plate.

Bo Jackson
Royals Outfielder
1986-90

"I'm about to throw a courtesy slide, and I see the ball in Bob Boone's mitt," said Reynolds. "I say, 'You've got to be kidding me.'"

As Frank White said in 2006, "That is the greatest throw I've ever seen in my baseball career."

Incidentally, the Royals scored two runs in the top of the 12th and won the game, 5-3.

7. *Brett Out Duels Gossage as Royals Reach*
Baseball's Promised Land, 1980

George Brett's two-out homer — after U.L. Washington reached on an infield single — that launched the Royals to the 1980 World Series against their long-time rivals, might be best summed up by Brett himself: "That, by far, was the biggest hit of my career. Ever. Especially after losing to them three straight years, 1976, '77 and '78. I give U.L. Washington a lot of credit for beating out the infield

single. It enabled me another at-bat, and I hit the first pitch into the upper deck. That was the best swing I ever took in my life."
(Editor's Note: See feature article at the beginning of this chapter.)

6. *Brett Hits Three Home Runs, Game 3 of 1978 ALCS*

With the best-of-five 1978 AL playoffs tied at 1-1, George Brett delivered a classic performance. Facing New York's Jim "Catfish" Hunter in the Bronx, Brett led off the game by knocking Hunter's second offering over the right-field wall. But he was far from finished. In the third inning, Brett gave the Royals a 2-1 lead when he hit another solo homer, this time into the seats in right. Then, with the Royals trailing 3-2, Brett led off the fifth inning with his third dinger.

If it weren't for Yankee catcher Thurman Munson's two-run home run in the bottom of the eighth inning that gave New York the decisive 6-5 lead, Brett's feat in Game 3 would be relived each October, whenever remarkable postseason highlights are shown. Instead, Brett's three-homer game against "Catfish" Hunter and the Yankees went down as just another incredible chapter in Brett's Hall of Fame career.

"It's too bad we didn't win it for George," said Royals starter Paul Splittorff. "He had one hell of a game."

5. *White Rat Out-Foxes Rival A's*

The date was Sept. 29, 1976. The Royals were in Oakland for the final game of a three-game set with the rival A's, whom they led in the standings by a mere 2½ games after dropping the first two matches in the series.

With regular catcher Buck Martinez and a couple of the club's stud pitchers ready for the all-important finale, manager Whitey Herzog made a shocking move by starting left-hander Larry Gura and catcher John Wathan.

Then there was outfielder Amos Otis, who had been beaned in the head two weeks earlier by Oakland pitcher Stan Bahnsen, and was benched for the first two games in Oakland. Herzog made sure Otis was in the lineup for the series finale.

Neither Gura nor Otis disappointed. Gura's four-hitter, combined with Otis' RBI double and two-run home run, led the Royals to a 4-0 victory. The win clinched at least a tie with the A's for the American League West title. The Royals went on to clinch the championship outright a few days later at home.

A LEGEND'S HIGH FIVE
FRED WHITE
Announcer

Fred White seemingly has done it all. For 25 years, he teamed with Denny Matthews on the Royals' radio broadcasts. He was a sportscaster in Topeka. He was one of the original play-by-play announcers on ESPN. He's broadcast for K-State, the University of Illinois, the ACC, and he's worked for Metro Sports. Besides announcing Big 12 basketball games, he's currently the Royals Director of Broadcast Services and Royals Alumni.

1. George Brett's home run off Rich "Goose" Gossage in the 1980 playoffs.

2. Dane Iorg's hit that won Game 6 of the 1985 World Series.

3. K-State's win over Russia in hoops in Ahearn Fieldhouse.

4. K-State vs. Missouri in football, 1970. Lynn Dickey was the quarterback for K-State. Missouri won the game, but it went down to the wire and finished as it got dark.

5. Final day of the Royals' 1976 season when five players in the game, including George Brett and Hal McRae, had a chance to win the A.L. batting championship. (Brett won it.)

Bonus pick:
   Opening of Royals Stadium in 1973, when Paul Splittorff shut out the Texas Rangers.

4. *Brett Pursues .400*

Although George Brett's average had been climbing the previous 28 games, during what turned out to be a 30-game hitting streak, this mid-August day was something fans never thought they'd see on the scoreboard: .401. Eclipsing .400 this late in the season was unheard of. Rod Carew passed .400 in 1977, but in early July.

It looked nearly impossible that Brett would go over .400 on this Sunday against Toronto, considering he went into the game batting

.394, needing a four-for-four performance. Even after three hits, there was no way he would hit in the eighth. Not with two outs and three batters ahead of him.

But sure enough, U.L. Washington beat out an infield grounder and Amos Otis walked. John Wathan was at the plate. Brett found himself in the on-deck circle with a .399 batting average.

"Wathan walked on four pitches, and with each ball, the crowd roared louder and louder," Brett remembered. "We were leaving town the next day, so I guess everybody wanted to see me get that next at-bat."

Blue Jays pitcher Mike Barlow, who had struck out Brett the previous night, entered the game. In typical Brett dramatics, he belted Barlow's fourth pitch over left fielder Garth Iorg's head for a bases-clearing double.

"The ovation was unbelievable," says Brett, who hit an amazing .494 for the month of July. "I looked around and saw what the average was and saw the standing ovation, so I just took my hat off and raised my arms up. It was special going over .400 at home. Little did I know what was going to happen over the next six weeks of the season."

September 19, 1980, marked Brett's final game at .400. During the season's last two weeks, his average dropped to .384, before he finished the year at .390. That was the highest average for a season since Ted Williams hit .406 in 1941. Since 1980, only Tony Gwynn has been higher. Gwynn finished the 1994 strike-shortened season at .394.

3. *Royals First-Ever Win*

On a cold day on April 8, 1969, the Royals inaugural game was tied at 3-3 in the 12th inning against Minnesota at Municipal Stadium. The bases were full of Royals after Twins manager Billy Martin called for intentional walks to Chuck Harrison and Bob Oliver. Joe Foy reached earlier on a single. Royals manager Joe Gordon, who had managed the Kansas City A's a few years earlier, called on Joe Keough, the club's hottest hitter during spring training, to pinch-hit for catcher Ellie Rodriguez. After Keough's great spring, during which he hit .350, it was thought that he'd be one of the starting outfielders. Instead, he was fresh in the 12th. He drove Dick

Woodson's first offering over right fielder Tony Oliva's head. Royals won 4-3.

"When I went up there, I was still a little irritated because I didn't start," Keough admitted 35 years later. "It was so cold, I just hit the first pitch as hard as I could. That definitely made my career highlight reel."

"Joe Keough hits a line drive to deep right field. Back goes Tony Oliva...it's over his head. Here comes the winning run, and the Royals win!"

— Denny Matthews' call of the Royals first win and his first game as a broadcaster

2. *The Pine Tar Game*

Just say the "pine tar game" and it brings visions of another classic contest between the Royals and the Yankees, a monster home run, an enraged George Brett, and another of the unique moments in Royals history.

The Yankees led the Royals 4-3 in the top of the ninth inning on July 24, 1983, at Yankee Stadium. With two outs, it was déjà vu all over again as U.L. Washington beat out an infield single that helped bring up Brett to face Yankee fireball closer "Goose" Gossage. And, just like Brett did during Game 3 of the 1980 ALCS, he hammered a Gossage fastball into the right-field seats.

Early in the series, Yankee third baseman Graig Nettles suggested to manager Billy Martin that Brett had too much pine tar on his bat. Brett's homer gave Martin the perfect opportunity to share his news with the umpires. The Royals sensed that Martin would draw attention to Brett's bat in a situation that mattered. So, as Brett rounded the bases, Royals hitting coach Rocky Colavito told pitcher Gaylord Perry to grab the bat.

"I got the bat from the umpire, and then several other teammates had it," Perry said. "We didn't want the Yankees or the umpires to get a hold of it. Finally, our tallest guy, pitcher Steve Renko (6-foot-5) got it and ran with it. There was a group of security guards waiting for Steve as he went up the runway."

The umpires did get the bat, and, as everyone remembers, after home plate umpire Tim McClelland and the rest of the crew messed around with it, they declared Brett out, beginning a tirade by Brett that hasn't been duplicated by another player since. Of course, Brett was ejected. As was Perry, who received a $250 fine for his part.

Three days later, American League President Lee MacPhail overturned the call.

The two teams finished the game on August 18 with a different umpiring crew. But, a prepared crew.

As Fred White wrote in *Play by Play*: "So the game resumed, and the Yankees threw to first base to protest, saying that George had missed first. Dave Phillips, one of the new umpires, pulls an affidavit out of his pocket that the umpiring crew that was there (in July) saw (Brett) touch first base. So the Yankees threw to second base. Here comes the affidavit from the previous crew saying that he touched second. That was when the Yankees got really frustrated. It was like, hell with it, go ahead and beat us and get on out of here."

The Royals did just that, winning 5-4.

1. *1985 World Series*

It stands to reason that the 1985 World Series, the moment voted No. 1 overall and the top sports win in the "history" of Kansas City sports, would be the top Royals moment, also.

Say what you want about "the call" at first base in Game 6 and how that may or may not have affected the outcome of the Series. Overall, Kansas City's win over the St. Louis Cardinals in seven games was a culmination of many factors coming together.

As expected, the club's star players, George Brett and Frank White, came up big during the Series. Brett hit .370 in the World Series with 10 hits and five runs, while White hit one of the club's two homers against the Cardinals, and led the Royals with six RBIs and three doubles. The club also received great performances from Willie Wilson, Lonnie Smith and Steve Balboni, all of whom hit better than .300 against the Cardinals.

And, despite being young and relatively inexperienced, the Royals pitching staff, led by 21-year-old Bret Saberhagen's 20 wins that season, did little wrong against the Cardinals. They held St. Louis to 13 runs and a .185 team batting average, the lowest-ever in a seven-game World Series. Saberhagen, the Series MVP, won two games and sported an amazing 0.50 ERA.

"We couldn't have asked (the pitching staff) to do more than they did," said then-General Manager John Schuerholz. "We built that team around pitching, defense and speed, and it paid off."

(Editor's Note: For more on the '85 World Series, see Chapter 1.)

Courtesy of the Kansas City Royals

**The Royals win the World Series,
Royals Stadium 1985**

FROM THE
TEXANS to THE TOP

Chapter 8

Kansas City, Kansas City Here We Come

K-A-N-S-A-S-C-I-T-Y-CHIEFS (Sung to the tune of the old Mickey Mouse Club, not the new Mickey Mouse Clubhouse.)

It seems preposterous today, considering the current popularity of the NFL, that at one time, not long ago, the Chiefs were seen as a Mickey Mouse outfit. Really, the NFL teams and its fans looked at every team in the original American Football League that way. Even the AFL owners, at the beginning of their existence, joked that they were "The Foolish Club" for entertaining the notion that they could compete with the NFL — on the field and in the books.

But there the Chiefs sat, in the Los Angeles Memorial Coliseum, ready to face the NFL's mighty Green Bay Packers in the first AFL-NFL World Championship Game.

Lamar Hunt desperately wanted to own a football team. He was in his early 20s and already a millionaire thanks to his father, oil man H.L. Hunt. In fact, early in the American Football League's existence, when Lamar Hunt was losing nearly a million dollars a year, a reporter asked H.L. how long Lamar could keep that up.

"Oh, maybe 150 years," H.L. quipped.

With his desire and nearly unlimited cash flow, Lamar Hunt contacted the NFL about granting him an expansion club in his hometown of Dallas. The NFL denied the request, but told him that the Chicago Cardinals could be for sale. Owner Walter Wolfner offered to make Hunt a minority owner at 20 percent. That wasn't good enough for Hunt, so he passed.

In 1959, after the NFL and the Cardinals had essentially shut the door on Hunt, the dreamer in him stepped up.

"Why wouldn't a second league work?" he wondered, realizing that baseball had its American and National Leagues. Why not football? That's all Hunt needed. He got the names of some of the other people who had contacted Wolfner about the Cardinals, and asked if they would be interested in forming a new league.

K.S. "Bud" Adams of Houston jumped at the opportunity. Two other groups — Bob Howsam in Denver, and Max Winter and Bill Boyer in Minnesota — also agreed. Not long after, Hunt also added Barron Hilton in Los Angeles and Harry Wismer in New York to the group to form the six-team American Football League. By the end of that year, before the teams drafted players, the league added franchises in Buffalo and Boston thanks to Ralph Wilson and Billy Sullivan, respectively.

Shortly before the initial November 22 draft, however, things almost unraveled for the new league. The Minnesota group pulled out, accepting an offer for a National Football League expansion team. (At the end of January 1960, the AFL awarded the franchise designated for Minnesota to an Oakland group headed by Chet Soda and Wayne Valley.) Then, the NFL came to Hunt about that expansion team that he had wanted to put in Dallas. Hunt returned the favor the NFL had extended to him in 1958 — he turned them down.

"(The AFL) was so important to me," Hunt said. "I had a lot of money in it, a lot invested in it. Emotionally, I spent a lot of time, effort and energy on it. ... (quitting) wouldn't have been the right thing to do."

Thus began the new league in which Hunt's Dallas Texans enjoyed relative success during their first two years, finishing second each season in the four-team West division. Then, in 1962, the Texans put together an 11-3 campaign and reached the AFL Championship game against in-state rival Houston.

Courtesy of AP Photo

Dallas Texan Coach Hank Stram gets a champagne shower in the dressing room after his Texans won the AFL championship by defeating the Houston Oilers 20-17, Dec. 24, 1962, in Houston.

During the season, though, Hunt felt he needed to move to another city. It was difficult for the team from the fledgling American Football League to compete for fan support with the NFL's Dallas Cowboys.

When Kansas City, Missouri, Mayor H. Roe Bartle caught wind of Hunt's desire, he immediately started courting. Bartle, nicknamed "The Chief," had tried to get pro football in Kansas City at least two other times, both with the AFL. The third time turned out to be a charm.

Hunt was concerned, however, that if anyone knew he was considering moving the team, it would be bad for the league and his Texans. Bartle guaranteed complete secrecy. Even when Hunt came to scout Kansas City as a possible location, only Bartle and his chauffeur knew Hunt was there. He flew to Kansas City under an assumed name, he checked in at the Muehlebach Hotel under an assumed name, and when Bartle had to introduce him to someone, he called him "Mr. Lamar."

"Although Hunt had made up his mind to move," Joe McGuff wrote in *Winning It All*, "his coaches and players were unaware of his decision as they began preparations for the league championship game."

Thanks to two touchdowns by Abner Haynes, the Texans jumped out to a 17-0 lead. They *eventually* won the game 20-17 on a 25-yard field goal by Tommy Brooker ... in the second overtime. By the time Brooker hit that kick, the two teams had played the longest professional football game ever, at 77 minutes, 54 seconds. (The game remains second on the all-time longest games list, behind, of course, the Chiefs-Dolphins Christmas Day contest in 1971.)

The exciting game and sudden-death double-overtime helped the nation see that the AFL was a legitimate and fun league.

And, just as Dallas was getting its first professional football championship, Hunt announced, on February 8, 1963, that he was moving the Texans to Kansas City if the city sold 25,000 season tickets. Three months later, on May 22, with just 13,025 season tickets sold, Hunt announced that he, indeed, was moving the franchise.

Although the move seemed great for Kansas City, the Texan players weren't so sure. Head coach Hank Stram had the unenviable task of convincing the players that moving north was a good thing.

"We went through quite a difficult transition because we were a Texas team," Stram said in 2001. "We signed players from Texas who wanted to be in Dallas. All of a sudden, we moved to Kansas City. It was traumatic because we had told our players that we would always be a Dallas team. When we decided to move, it ruffled the emotions of a lot of guys.

"However, once we got to Kansas City, it didn't take long to fall in love with the city and the people. We were always so appreciative of the support we got from the fans in Kansas City, and how involved they were with our football team. They really responded to what we were doing.

"As we went along, we grew and developed, not only as a football team, but also as a community. Growing as a community was very important for all of us involved in the transition."

The move gave many players, such as wide receiver Chris Burford, who had just purchased a new home in Dallas and was attending law school there, a new place to call home. Even if they weren't thrilled in the beginning.

"Going to Kansas City was a *big* surprise to the players," he said. "It was tough going from the Cotton Bowl to old Municipal Stadium, which was an old baseball park. The first year, we didn't have many people show up. In our first exhibition game, there were less than 10,000 people there (5,721), which was embarrassing."

The team changed its nickname to the Chiefs — largely in honor of Mayor Bartle, and the Kansas City climate provided a memorable experience for those players from Texas. Although they had played games in places like Boston and New York in November and December, their new home wasn't as warm as Dallas.

"The last three games (that first year), we played in 12-15 below zero," said E.J. Holub, whom Stram nicknamed "The Holler Guy." "That turf felt like concrete. The 1,000 fans there were either in bedrolls or drunk. After that, we really got going."

(Truth told, in those final three games in 1963, all at home, the Chiefs averaged a little better than 14,000 fans.)

"The town changed over time," Burford added. "It became much more sophisticated about professional football. The fan base grew and the fans got behind us. Then, in 1966, which was a fabulous season, we landed in Kansas City after beating Buffalo in the AFL Championship game and the fans surged onto the runway. It was a very exciting time for us as players."

Hank Stram was a master motivator. He knew exactly which buttons to push and when. So, in spite of the pressure on his Chiefs as the first representative from the AFL to play in a championship game against the NFL, facing the powerhouse from Green Bay no less, Stram tried to lighten up his team's mood before the game.

"I asked our equipment manager to go to the five-and-dime store and get some Mickey Mouse ears and the Mickey Mouse theme song," Stram said. "When the players walked into the locker room, the equipment guys were wearing the Mickey Mouse ears, while the theme song played in the background. I thought, 'What the hell; we'll have a little fun with this and maybe get them relaxed to play like they're supposed to play.'"

The players certainly seemed to be a little relaxed. Heck, they were giddy.

Second-year receiver Frank Pitts, who played mainly on special teams for the Chiefs in Super Bowl I remembered: "Before the game I ran by (Green Bay coach Vince) Lombardi on the sidelines and started rambling, 'I've seen you on TV so much and I'm out here in Los Angeles, and...' and I shook his hand. He said, 'It's great to have you out here, now get back to the other side.'

"Then, on the kickoff, I made the tackle on Elijah Pitts. When I got him, I was hugging him and falling to the ground and I said,

'This is your namesake making a tackle!' He said, 'Fine, get up.' That was a big highlight for me. ... (The game) was so new that anything and everything was exciting."

Defeating the Bills 31-7 on January 1, 1967 (the very day future Kansas City star Derrick Thomas was born) for the AFL Championship, however, gave the Chiefs a belief that they belonged on the same field as the Packers. It also didn't hurt that the Chiefs scored more than 30 points in eight of their 14 regular-season games. In four of those, they scored at least 40.

"Even though the Packers were favored going into that game," Stram said, "we never felt like we were the underdog."

Still, the Chiefs knew they'd have to rely heavily on their offense if they were going to beat Green Bay. Kansas City's defense wasn't the team's strength, and the team knew it might not provide a worthy opponent to quarterback Bart Starr and his potent Packer offense.

As the Chiefs had hoped, they kept things close in the first half, trailing 14-10 at the break. However, their concern came to fruition: they couldn't slow down Green Bay's offense in the second half. The Packers went on to win 35-10, as Starr threw for 250 yards and two touchdowns on 16-for-23 passing.

"One thing about playing in a Super Bowl game is that if you have any shortcomings, they're going to be exposed," Stram said. "(Defense) was our shortcoming.

"(Super Bowl I) did provide us with a lot of impetus that we wanted to make it back to that championship (game) again, and if we did make it back, we would win."

Chapter 9

Top Chiefs Players and Moments

TOP 10 CHIEFS PLAYERS

10t. *Marcus Allen, Running Back, 1993-97*

After spending the first 11 years of his career with the Raiders, where he was the MVP of Super Bowl XVIII, Marcus Allen joined the Chiefs prior to the 1993 season. In 1995, against the Raiders of all teams, Allen became the first player in NFL history to gain more than 10,000 yards rushing and 5,000 yards receiving. (He also scored

Marcus Allen

his 100th touchdown against the Raiders.) The next year, on Thanksgiving Day, Allen broke Walter Payton's all-time rushing touchdown record of 110. By the time he retired in '97, Allen racked up 12,243 rushing yards, 5,411 receiving yards, and 145 touchdowns (123 rushing). Without question, Marcus Allen is one of the best running backs in the history of football and possibly the best third-and-short and goal-line rusher the NFL has ever seen.

10t. *Jan Stenerud, Kicker, 1967-79*

Every once in a while, a player comes along and revolutionizes his position. Norway native Jan Stenerud, attending Montana State on a skiing scholarship, did just that with the kicking game in pro football. Montana State's basketball coach discovered Stenerud kicking field goals at the football stadium. Although he wasn't the first soccer-style kicker, Stenerud became proof that kicking the football soccer-style could be fortuitous. At least it was for the Chiefs. During his 13 seasons with Kansas City, Stenerud scored 1,231 points on 279 field goals and 394 extra points. In 1991, Stenerud became the first true place-kicker to be inducted into the Pro Football Hall of Fame.

9. *Otis Taylor, Wide Receiver, 1965-75*

If there's one former Chiefs player who hasn't received his due from the Pro Football Hall of Fame, it has to be Otis Taylor. During his pro career, the 6'3" Taylor was one of the first pro receivers to use the lethal combination of size, speed, athletic ability and great hands. Unquestionably, he was one of the top wide receivers during his era. Playing in 130 games for the Chiefs, Taylor amassed 7,306 receiving yards on 410 receptions, with 57 touchdown catches, and 20 games with 100 or more yards. His 46-yard touchdown play helped lead the Chiefs to victory over the Vikings in Super Bowl IV.

8. *Willie Lanier, Linebacker, 1967-77*

Along with Bobby Bell and Jim Lynch, Willie Lanier helped form one of the greatest linebacker corps in NFL history. From the middle linebacker position, Lanier also was one of the most feared tacklers in the NFL. Similar to Bell, Lanier intercepted 27 passes during his career and recovered 15 fumbles.

The one game that probably best sums up Lanier's fire and ability came during the first round of the 1969 playoffs, on the road against the defending world champion New York Jets. In the fourth quarter, with the Chiefs leading 6-3, the Jets had the ball on the Kansas City 1-yard-line on first down after a pass interference call against the Chiefs. The Chiefs went on to win the game 13-6, and eventually reached Super Bowl IV against the Minnesota Vikings.

7. Buck Buchanan, Defensive Tackle, 1963-75

After an incredible season by quarterback Len Dawson in 1962, the Chiefs felt they could trade their previous signal-caller, Cotton Davidson, for the number-one draft pick. They did just that and selected Buck Buchanan, a ferocious lineman out of Grambling. During his 13-year pro career, the 6'7", 295-pound Buchanan missed only one game. He also recorded the first sack in Super Bowl history, taking down Green Bay quarterback Bart Starr in Super Bowl I.

Buck Buchanan's final appearance at Arrowhead Stadium came during an on-field ceremony in 1990 to accept his Pro Football Hall of Fame ring. Already sick with cancer at that time, Buchanan lost the battle on July 16, 1992. He was 51.He learned the Chiefs were retiring his Number 86 shortly before he passed away.

6. Priest Holmes, Running Back, 2001-06*

Just a few years after Marcus Allen retired, the Chiefs acquired another running back who had been tossed aside by his former team. This time it was Priest Holmes, whom the Baltimore Ravens didn't feel they needed with Jamal Lewis in the backfield. Ravens' loss, Chiefs' gain. Holmes burst onto the scene for the Chiefs with a then-record 1,555 rushing yards in his first season, a season that earned his first Pro Bowl berth. Although injuries have nagged Holmes during his time with the Chiefs, he still holds several team records including rushing yards (5,933), touchdowns (83), rushing touchdowns (76) and 100-yard rushing games (24). Holmes is the only player in Chiefs history to record more than 100 yards rushing and 100 yards receiving in two games.

5. Hank Stram, Head Coach, 1960-74

Hank Stram

Hank Stram, who was known as "The Mentor," began with the Chiefs organization in 1960 — the first year of the American Football League — when the team was known as the Dallas Texans. For the next 15 years, he was instrumental in the team's success. He molded players, helped the organization move to Kansas City, helped the team make

* Signed with Chiefs through 2009

a smooth merger to the NFL ... oh, and he won. A lot. In fact, with Stram at the helm, the Chiefs won three AFL titles and went to two Super Bowls, winning the world championship in Super Bowl IV. During Stram's 15 seasons with the Chiefs, he won 124 games, lost 76 and tied 10. After his coaching career, he went on to become a top NFL analyst for CBS Sports, widely known for his radio work with Jack Buck on Monday night games. Stram, who was inducted into the Pro Football Hall of Fame in 2003, died on July 4, 2005, at the age of 82.

4. Bobby Bell, Linebacker, 1963-74

Bobby Bell could seemingly do it all. And, before joining the Chiefs as a seventh-round selection in the 1963 AFL draft, he did do it all at the University of Minnesota. Recruited as a running back out of high school in North Carolina, Bell switched to quarterback during his freshman year for the Gophers. By the time he won the Outland Trophy in 1962 as the nation's top lineman, Bell played center and tackle on both sides of the ball. It even took the Chiefs a couple seasons to decide where to put him. Originally a defensive end for the first two years of his pro career, Bell moved to outside linebacker where he became one of the best in the history of the NFL. During 168 career games, Bell intercepted 26 passes for 479 yards and recovered 15 fumbles. In 1983, Bell became the first Chiefs player to be enshrined in the Pro Football Hall of Fame.

3. Len Dawson, Quarterback, 1962-75

It could be said that Len Dawson was destined to be a quarterback. That really seems to be the most logical reason he went from a hesitant 125-pound fifth-string quarterback during his sophomore year in high school — with more passion and ability to play baseball and basketball — to an NFL Hall of Famer. Dawson, who played collegiate ball at Purdue after being recruited by one of their assistant coaches named Hank Stram, spent five years in the NFL with Pittsburgh and Cleveland. In 1962, with his Dallas Texans needing a quarterback, Stram went after Dawson.

It paid off immediately. Dawson led the Chiefs to the AFL championship that season en route to becoming the league's Player of the Year by *The Sporting News*. "Lenny the Cool" led the Chiefs to Super Bowls I and IV, winning the MVP award after the Chiefs' victory over Minnesota. He finished his career with 28,507 yards and 237 touchdown passes. Dawson, whose Number 16 was retired by the Chiefs, finally was inducted into the Pro Football Hall of Fame in 1987.

2. *Fred Arbanas, Tight End, 1962-70*

During his nine-year career with the Dallas Texans-Kansas City Chiefs, Fred Arbanas solidified himself as one of the best tight ends in pro football. In 118 games, Arbanas, whom the Texans drafted in the seventh round of the 1961 AFL draft, caught 198 passes for 3,101 yards and 34 touchdowns. Arbanas was a five-time All-AFL performer, even the season after he lost the sight in his left eye due to an attack by a stranger in December 1964. Although partial vision has been restored, Arbanas played the rest of his career blind in that eye. The Pro Football Hall of Fame selected Arbanas in 1970 for the all-time AFL team.

1. *Derrick Thomas, Linebacker, 1989-99*

Dominating. That might be the best way to describe Derrick Thomas, the Chiefs first-round draft pick (fourth overall) in 1989. During his 11-year career, Thomas became a menacing pass rusher, recording a team-record 126.5 sacks. He set the NFL record for sacks in a game in 1990, when he got to Seattle's Dave Krieg seven times. He then tied for second on the single-game list in 1998, when he recorded six sacks against the Oakland Raiders.

On January 2, 2000, Thomas became the first Chiefs player to play in a regular season game in three decades.

Tragically, Thomas died a month later, on February 8, 2000, a little more than two weeks after being seriously injured in single-vehicle accident on Interstate 435.

(Editor's Note: For more about Derrick Thomas, see feature article in next chapter.)

"A Fan's View"

"Growing up, I totally lived the Chiefs. My dad was an absolute live-and-die Chiefs fan. Chiefs games were something that pulled us together. In the pre-sellout days of the 1970s, when the Chiefs were playing at home but we couldn't watch them on TV in Kansas City, my dad would want to watch the Chiefs so badly that sometimes we would drive down to La Cygne, Kansas, and park our trailer on the top of a hill and hope that we could get the UHF signal from Joplin, Missouri. If we didn't, Dad would drive another hour and a half south, and we'd just show up at my Uncle Dave and Aunt Kathy's house in Pittsburg, Kansas, to watch a game with them.

"I can't remember much that I did with my dad as a kid — I can't remember him taking me to a single Royals game, I don't remember a particular movie that he took me to — but I vividly remember December 1973, when Dad took me to a game at Arrowhead and we sat in the end zone. The wind chill was 20-below and we had a Hefty bag on our legs to help knock out the wind. I thought that was the greatest thing I had ever done. I still remember that like it was yesterday. So, for me, even cheering for the team during the 1987 strike season was a privilege because it was my team, and a great bond for Dad and me."

— Steve Beaumont, Chiefs yell leader, 1986-87

TOP 10 CHIEFS MOMENTS

10. *Deron Cherry Picks Off the Raiders Twice in Arrowhead's First Playoff Game, 1991*

The Chiefs' first playoff game in Arrowhead Stadium was also Deron Cherry's last home game. The game was a result of something that happened a week earlier, when the Chiefs went to Los Angeles and beat the Raiders, bringing the playoffs to Kansas City for the first time since 1971. Despite the outcome of the game in L.A., Raiders quarterback Todd Marinovich lit up the Chiefs secondary. Cherry didn't want to experience that in his final game at Arrowhead.

"I stayed in the film room all week to figure out Marinovich, trying to find an edge on him," Cherry said.

It must have worked. On Marinovich's first pass of the playoff game, Cherry was there for the interception. On the Raiders' next offensive series, Cherry again picked off a Marinovich pass. During the Chiefs 10-6 win that day, in addition to his two picks, Cherry led the team in tackles with seven.

A LEGEND'S HIGH FIVE
DERON CHERRY
Chiefs Safety, 1981-91

1. 1991 Playoff game vs. Raiders. That was our first playoff game at Arrowhead, and I wound up with two interceptions. That also was my last game at Arrowhead.

2. 1986 regular-season finale at Pittsburgh. We had beaten Denver and won at the Raiders the previous two weeks, and we had to beat the Steelers to go to the playoffs. We won 24-19, with all of our points on special teams and field goals. We scored on a blocked punt return, a field goal, a kickoff return and a blocked field goal return. That was our first trip to the playoffs.

3. Four interceptions against Seattle. The interesting thing is that I had my hands on nine balls even though it rained the whole game. I had a fifth interception in my hands but my own guy, Lloyd Burruss, knocked it out.

4. Monday Night Football game in 1991 against Buffalo. It was the first one at Arrowhead (since 1983). The atmosphere was electric. That's when Arrowhead started becoming recognized as the loudest stadium in league. On top of that, the game wasn't even close. We won 33-6.

5. The games when I got my first interception and my 50th interception. The first was against the Raiders in 1981. The 50th, which was my last one, came against Seattle in 1991.

BONUS:
The November 1990 game against the Raiders. I had been out 10 months because of knee surgery. Kevin Porter came up to me before the game and said he had a dream about me the night before, that on my first play of the game, I would hit the running back, he would fumble and I would recover it. On the first play I got in there, Bo Jackson was carrying the ball. I knocked it loose and we recovered. The person I saw after the play was Kevin, so I ran over to give him a high five and he ran away from me as if he'd just seen a ghost.

9. *Joe Montana Over John Elway on Monday Night Football, October 17, 1994*

In what many consider to be one of the greatest games in Monday Night Football history, Hall of Famer Joe Montana finished with 393 yards and three touchdowns on 34-of-54 passing, out dueling fellow Hall of Famer John Elway, who went 18-of-29 for 263 yards and two touchdowns.

The game at Denver's Mile High Stadium is best remembered for Montana's game-winning drive, which ended when he found receiver Willie Davis at the front corner of the end zone with 8 seconds remaining. The play capped off an 81-second, 75-yard drive that gave the Chiefs a 31-28 victory.

It was the Chiefs' first win in Denver since the strike-shortened season of 1982, Montana's first win at Mile High Stadium in four tries, and coach Marty Schottenheimer's first win in Denver in eight attempts.

8. *Chiefs Beat Houston in 1993 AFC Divisional Playoff Game*

The Chiefs rallied for 21 points at the Astrodome behind future Hall of Fame players Joe Montana and Marcus Allen. After Montana threw two touchdown passes, Allen sealed the 28-20 win for Kansas City.

"I was watching the game from the end zone," said Chiefs President/General Manager Carl Peterson. "We got down to the 21-yard line, and Joe took a snap, turned and handed the ball to Marcus. When Joe turned around — before Marcus had even hit the line of scrimmage — he threw his arms up signaling 'touchdown.' Then Marcus made about three moves and took it to the left corner of the end zone for the score. I asked Joe later (why he raised his arms so early). He said, 'I saw the man who's got the best vision there is, and he took it.'"

And the Chiefs were headed to the AFC Championship game.

7. *Montana and Allen Lead Chiefs to '93 AFC Title Game*

An old quarterback beyond his prime and some washed-up Heisman Trophy winner. That was the thought when the Chiefs signed quarterback Joe Montana and running back Marcus Allen before the 1993 season. After all, Montana was 37 years old and Allen had been spending time on the bench with the Raiders, people assuming his career was finished. Instead, the two gave Kansas City fans some extra excitement heading into the season and led the team to the conference championship game at Buffalo. There, however, it was Buffalo running back Thurman Thomas taking over the game with 186 yards and three touchdowns as the Bills won 30-13. Montana suffered a concussion early in the third quarter, with the Chiefs trailing 20-6. Kansas City's lone touchdown of the game, though, came from Allen, who capped a 90-yard drive with a 1-yard scoring run.

Montana played one more year with the Chiefs before retiring. Allen, the NFL's Comeback Player of the Year in '93, played until the end of the 1997 season.

6. *"The Brawl"*

"Anytime we played (the Raiders), we knew there'd be a fight at some point," said former Chiefs great E.J. Holub.

But, there is one fight in the rivalry between the Chiefs and Raiders that stands out above the rest in terms of timing and importance. It was on November 1, 1970, at Municipal Stadium. At the time, the Chiefs, the Raiders and the Denver Broncos were duking it out for the top spot in the division.

The Chiefs led the Raiders 17-14 near midfield with 1 minute, 8 seconds left. On third down, quarterback Len Dawson ran for 19 yards on a bootleg. While Dawson was on the ground, face down, Oakland's Ben Davidson literally spearheaded Dawson in the back with a vicious and extremely late hit. When Davidson stood up,

Chiefs wide receiver Otis Taylor grabbed Davidson by the neck and threw him to the ground. The benches cleared and it took several minutes to restore order. Taylor was ejected and the Chiefs were penalized, negating the first down.

"I have to admit that I wasn't surprised when Otis did that, because he was that type of player. He was protecting me," said Dawson. "It also didn't surprise me that once Otis jumped on Davidson, the rest of our teammates jumped in there, too."

The Raiders got the ball back on a punt, marched just beyond midfield, and kicker George Blanda hit a 48-yard field goal for the game-ending tie. The outcome of the game, combined with a Denver loss earlier in the day, put the Raiders in first, Denver in second and the Chiefs in third. They ended the season a few weeks later, 7-5-2.

"A Fan's View"

"A story that comes to mind happened during a Chiefs-Raiders game from my first year as a yell leader. There was a pay phone just outside our locker room. At halftime, Oakland's Howie Long  called someone — we were guessing his wife — from that phone. With full pads on, Howie practically filled the hallway. None of us dared pass because, from the tone of his voice, he was pretty ticked off. When he finished, he slammed down the phone and looked for something to **Steve Beaumont** take out his fury on. Luckily for me, the big portable kerosene heater was closer to him than I was. Have you ever seen one of those heaters? They're not small. But neither is Howie Long. He absolutely laid into it as if it were a football. He kicked it all the way out to the tunnel. He turned around and caught eyes with me with a look so fiery that I thought my polyester uniform would combust. He growled: 'What the *#&! are you lookin' at?' In my best manly tone, I called up the courage to answer: 'Nothing.' What a man I was! But, I am really glad I didn't have to line up in front of Howie during the second half. I pity the guy who did."

— Steve Beaumont, Chiefs yell leader, 1986-87

5. *Derrick Thomas Sacks Seattle QB Seven Times*

If there ever was a day when Derrick Thomas looked possessed on the field, it would be Veteran's Day, 1990, during Thomas' second season in the NFL. Appropriately, on a day when Americans pay honor to those who served our country, Thomas had his father Robert on his mind. Robert Thomas was an Air Force captain whose plane was shot down during the Vietnam War in a mission called "Operation: Linebacker Two." (He was declared dead in 1980.) DT went out and set a single-game record by sacking Seattle quarterback Dave Krieg seven times. On the final play of the game, Thomas had Krieg in his grasp for what would have been an eighth sack, but Krieg broke loose and threw a game-winning touchdown.

4. *Dante Hall Sets Kick Return Touchdown Record*

The Chiefs hadn't seen anyone as electric — or as small — since Noland "Super Gnat" Smith. But in 2003, Dante Hall proved that speed and quickness and athletic ability can outdo size any day of the week. That year, the 5-foot-8, 187-pound Hall became the first player in NFL history to return a kick or punt for a touchdown in four consecutive games. It started innocently enough with a 100-yard kickoff return against Pittsburgh on September 14. The next week, Hall switched it up and returned a punt 73 yards against Houston. Then, a 97-yard kickoff return at Baltimore that turned out to be the deciding touchdown. Hall's fourth, which was his most spectacular, was a dizzying 93-yard punt return that helped lead the Chiefs past rival Denver. One side note — in an AFC playoff game against Indianapolis three months after the return against the Broncos, Hall returned a kickoff 92 yards for a touchdown. With that, he became the first player in NFL history to return five kicks or punts for touchdowns in the same season, when including the playoffs.

3. *Death of Derrick Thomas*

(Editor's Note: See feature article in next chapter)

2. *Priest Holmes Breaks NFL Touchdown Record*

As if Dante Hall's electrifying play wasn't enough for Chiefs fans in 2003, they got a treat through running back Priest Holmes, who racked up an NFL single-season record 27 rushing touchdowns. On December 28, Holmes scored his final two touchdowns of the season against Chicago. With the first, number 26 on the year, he passed Dallas' Emmitt Smith for the single-season rushing touchdown record. The second gave him the single-season record for total touchdowns, passing Marshall Faulk; and he passed Chiefs legend Otis Taylor for most touchdowns (61) in team history. Two years after Holmes set the NFL standard, Seattle's Shaun Alexander ran for 28 touchdowns.

1. *Super Bowl IV*

In case you missed the feature article on the game in Chapter 2, here's a recap: the Chiefs beat the Minnesota Vikings 23-7 in the final AFL-NFL Championship game, or what's known today as Super Bowl IV.

"Where Have You Gone?"

FRANK PITTS

Frank Pitts has wonderful memories from his time with the Kansas City Chiefs. Great teammates. Trips to Super Bowls I and IV. Being part of the American Football League's breakthrough. Sadly, though, in December 2005, burglars took two of Pitts' prized mementos from his career: his two Super Bowl rings.

"They trashed our room," said Pitts, who lives in Baton Rouge, Louisiana, with Diane, his wife of more than 40 years. "They went into our computer room and didn't take anything. They also didn't take anything from our front room, which is where I have pictures and paraphernalia from my days (in the NFL)."

Pitts, who's a sergeant-at-arms in the Louisiana Senate, had been wearing the rings as the senators with whom he works were traveling to areas affected by Hurricane Katrina. Some of the senators felt that it would be enjoyable for their constituents to see the rings. Something to take their minds briefly off the overwhelming tasks at hand.

For reasons unknown even to Pitts, he decided to leave the rings at home one December day. He put them in their normal resting place, ring boxes in the second drawer of his bedroom dresser. Later that morning, burglars kicked in the back door of Pitts' home. A television, VCR and DVD player were taken, along with some other jewelry.

But the stolen rings meant the most. In fact, if necessary, Pitts said he will pay the $10,746 to have two new rings made using the original molds.

"The only reason I want them back is for my son, who's done so well in his life," said Pitts, who began working for the Louisiana legislature around 2001, after spending most of his post-playing career as a physical education and special education teacher. "I want (the rings) to be part of the legacy that I leave for him."

During 1965-71, Pitts was a speedy receiver whom the Chiefs picked in the fourth round of the 1965 American Football League draft out of Southern in Baton Rouge. The Chiefs chose two other receivers with speed in that draft, Otis Taylor and Gloster Richardson. (Incidentally, the Chiefs first pick was former Kansas star Gale Sayers, who decided to play for the NFL's Chicago Bears.)

The threesome came along at a time when the 40-yard dash was first being recorded on a regular basis. Pitts, the speediest of the three, clocked a 4.4. That speed led to one of the Chiefs most effective plays during their Super Bowl seasons.

"(Coach Hank Stram) got excited when he saw how quick I was in a short distance, and came up with a reverse," says Pitts. "We mastered it during the 1966 season, when we went to the first Super Bowl. Then we perfected it two years later."

That season, 1968, was Pitts' best season statistically. He ended with 107 rushing yards on 11 carries, and 655 receiving yards and six touchdowns on 30 catches.

The next season, the Chiefs reached Super Bowl IV in New Orleans. Pitts was fired up. After all, it was close to where he attended college in Baton Rouge, plus Southern's marching band played at halftime. Besides, the Chiefs as a team wanted to repeat the New York Jets' showing in Super Bowl III, proving that the AFL was for real.

"We were determined to let everybody know we were going to take care of business," Pitts said. "I was plum excited, and I tried to show off."

Did he ever. Two reverses to Pitts and another long pass play set up Kansas City points — two Jan Stenerud field goals and a Taylor touchdown. Pitts finished with 37 yards rushing and 33 yards receiving. The Chiefs manhandled the Vikings, 23-7.

"In Super Bowl IV, we still had that shadow of the 'Mickey Mouse League' following us around," says Pitts, referring to the AFL's nickname. "But we went out and proved that we were bigger and better."

Before the next season, the AFL and NFL merged.

As Pitts looks at his NFL career, which ended before the 1975 season after shorter stops in Cleveland and Oakland, he's especially mindful of his first season in Kansas City, which led to two Super Bowl appearances.

"I just got in there in '65 and made my way," he says. "I worked for it, but I got lucky."

Chapter 10

So Long, DT

*"I miss the friend and brother in him the most.
And his smile. He was a happy, fun guy to be
around. Nobody can take his place."*

Neil Smith knows about heartbreak. You could say he felt it professionally after the Chiefs lost six times in the playoffs during his career, including the 1993 AFC Championship game. That pain goes away.

More importantly, though, Smith certainly felt it — and still feels it — after the unexpected death of his former teammate and best friend, Derrick Thomas. It's a pain that never will go away completely.

"I think about him every day," Smith said. "There's not a day that he doesn't cross my mind. I sometimes ask myself, what would Derrick do in this situation."

The hurt for Smith, the Chiefs family and anyone with a heart, really, started on Sunday afternoon, January 23, 2000. While enroute to the airport to go to St. Louis for the NFC Championship game on a snowy and icy Interstate-435, Thomas lost control of his Chevy Suburban, hit a median and caromed out of control. Thomas and one of his passengers, Mike Tellis, were ejected from the vehicle. Thomas suffered a fractured neck and a fractured back. Tellis died at the scene. Neither was wearing his seatbelt. Another passenger, John Hagebusch, who was buckled up, suffered minor injuries.

The next day, paralyzed from the neck down, Thomas was taken to one of the nation's top spinal research centers at Jackson Memorial Hospital in Miami, his hometown.

Through reports almost daily on TV, radio and *The Kansas City Star*, fans were told of Thomas' status and reminded of his long road toward recovery. Carl Peterson had visited Thomas — Peterson's first draft pick who had become like a son to the Chiefs GM — on February 7 at the hospital.

"I stepped out in the hall and coming down the hall was Derrick Thomas, in a wheelchair, but upbeat," Peterson said at the time. "I said, 'Son, you're mobile.' And he said, 'Father, I am. I've got wheels.'"

"Derrick was in such a better mood, very optimistic about his life ahead," Peterson said in 2005. "I remember flying back to Kansas City the night before with (Chiefs doctor) Jon Browne, and we were truly amazed at Derrick's spirit and determination."

But something went horribly wrong. At 10:10 Eastern Standard Time the next morning, Thomas died from a pulmonary embolism — a blood clot that lodged in an artery between his heart and a lung. He was 33.

The Chiefs family has suffered unexpected losses during the organization's existence: Stone Johnson, Mack Lee Hill and Joe Delaney. But this one hurt a little more.

On the field, Thomas, the Chiefs first pick in 1989, quickly became a fan favorite. With an incredible quickness, grace and tenacity, he bullied offensive linemen and quarterbacks. Leading a renaissance of the Chiefs defense, he reminded long-time Chiefs fans of the great linebackers of the past such as Bobby Bell and Willie Lanier.

In his rookie season, Thomas recorded 13 tackles (six solo) in a game at Cleveland. Almost a year to the date later, he had a career-defining game when he sacked Seattle quarterback Dave Krieg seven times, setting an NFL single-game record. During his 11-year career in which he went to nine Pro Bowls, Thomas set Chiefs records with 45 forced fumbles, 19 fumble recoveries, three safeties and four touchdowns.

Thomas teamed with Neil Smith, the team's top pick in '88, and formed one of pro football's all-time best defensive tandems. Opponents couldn't focus on one and not the other.

"We felt we put the seven-step drop out of football," Smith said. "They dropped it down to three steps and now it's one step. We felt we helped change a lot of (tactics)."

Thomas and Smith accounted for 184.5 sacks between them. Smith finished his Kansas City career with 86.5 sacks. He's second on the team's all-time list behind Thomas, who had 126.5 in his career following the 1999 season.

On and off the field, Smith and Thomas were inseparable.

"We kept each other out of trouble," Smith says.

As Metro Sports' Dave Stewart pointed out in his "Eat This" column on the station's Web site after Smith's induction into the Chiefs Hall of Fame on October 22, 2006: "They were Frick and Frack from the start."

They were like a couple of big kids. Both always smiling and cutting up. Adhering themselves to a city that was in the midst of going football crazy. Of course, acting like a big kid got Thomas in trouble a few times, privately and publicly. His play on the field, though, helped fans overlook his orneriness.

But, like most dynamic duos — Simon and Garfunkel, Elvis and Priscilla, Shaq and Kobe — Smith and Thomas separated, when Smith signed with Denver after the 1996 season.

"Once we split up, I always said in my mind that Derrick made me what I was and I feel I was a key part in his career," said Smith. "But, I never took over a ballgame. He could take over a game."

Even so, Smith helped the Broncos reach the Super Bowl, while Thomas' stock as a star athlete in the Kansas City community continued to rise. His name oftentimes was mentioned in the same breath as George Brett and Tom Watson.

"He was a presence wherever he was," Smith said. "I told him that he was the only guy I knew that when a President was in the city, he could get out of practice to go shake the President's hand, while the rest of us had to practice."

Indeed, the first President George Bush designated Thomas as his 832nd "Point of Light" for Thomas' work in the Kansas City community. The two met when President Bush was in Kansas City on September 11, 1992. In 1993, the NFL bestowed its highest honor on Thomas when the league selected him as the Edge NFL Man of the Year, which mainly takes into account a player's service in the community.

Thomas served on numerous boards for non-profit groups and he took on countless charitable endeavors.

"On-the-field accolades are great," Thomas once said, "but in order to reach your full potential, you have to overstep the boundaries of football and go out into the community and be an All-Pro there, too."

Even today, Derrick Thomas' legacy lives on through his "Third and Long Foundation," which he established in 1990 as an inner-city reading program to fight illiteracy.

"I had to overcome a language disability, so when he told me that he wanted to fight illiteracy, I knew it was a great (cause)," said Smith. "He asked me to help him come up with a name. A few days later, I asked him what his favorite down and distance was. We came up with 'Third and Long,' and he lit up like a Christmas tree."

Smith now spearheads the foundation which has been renamed the "Derrick Thomas/Neil Smith Third and Long Foundation."

It's a way for Smith to help carry on Derrick Thomas' work and help fill the tremendous void left brought by Thomas' death.

"I miss the friend and brother in him the most. And his smile. He was a happy, fun guy to be around," Smith said. "Nobody can take his place."

Derrick Thomas
1967 - 2000

Picture courtesy of AP Graphics

◆◆◆◆◆◆◆◆◆◆ Section IV ◆◆◆◆◆◆◆◆◆

BALLS and PUCKS and GOALS, OH MY

Chapter 11

The Best of the Other Pros

BASKETBALL
TOP 10 KINGS

The Kings came to Kansas City, bringing NBA basketball for the first time, in 1972. The Kings spent their first two seasons splitting time between Omaha and Kansas City. After coming to Kansas City exclusively during 1974-75, the Kings played their final game on April 14, 1985, before moving to Sacramento, California.

10. Reggie Theus
9. Joe C. Meriweather
8. Eddie Johnson
7. Sam Lacey
6. Larry Drew
5. Phil Ford
4. Scott Wedman
3. Cotton Fitzsimmons
2. Otis Birdsong
1. Nate "Tiny" Archibald

A LEGEND'S HIGH-5
SCOTT WEDMAN
Kansas City Kings Forward
1975-81

1. Playoffs in 1975. It was the first time the team wasn't in Omaha part-time, and the first time the franchise went to the playoffs in eight years.

2. Winning Midwest Division in 1979. We beat the Los Angeles Lakers late in the year to lock up the division.

3. Kemper Arena roof collapsing after a storm. It was a lowlight right after the 1979 season but it was important because we

had been averaging about 10,000 fans. We went back to Municipal Auditorium to play our games, and we lost some of our fan base.

4. Playoffs in 1981. We finished 40-42, but we kept winning in the playoffs and reached the Conference Finals against Houston. That was quite an accomplishment because we won up at Portland and then we won at Phoenix.

5. Cotton Fitzsimmons became the head coach in 1978. That was a great turning point for the team.

HOCKEY
TOP 10 SCOUTS

Whether because of the team's short stay or by the fans' choice, not many people remember the two seasons when the National Hockey League called Kansas City home with the expansion Scouts in 1974-75. So, this was one of the few top-10 lists that fans didn't choose. Instead, a seemingly unlikely source generated this list: Royals broadcaster Denny Matthews, who has a passion for hockey and is a former Scouts season-ticket holder. Matthews, who has played hockey since the 1960s, had the chance to skate with a few of the Scouts during their brief stop in Kansas City before, eventually, becoming the current New Jersey Devils. Since many of the Scouts either had been good players before arriving in Kansas City, or got better after they left, Matthews' list is in alphabetical order.

10. Phil Roberto
9. Wilf Paiement
8. Simon Nolet*
("probably the team's best player")
7. Brent Hughes
6. Denis Herron*
5. Larry Giroux
4. Denis Dupere
3. Guy Charron*
2. Gary Bergman
1 Chuck Arnason*

* indicates the players who were probably the best Scouts

TOP 10 BLADES

One of the more successful minor-league teams to call Kansas City home, the Blades played in the International Hockey League from 1990 to 2001. In 1992, the Blades won the Turner Cup championship.

10. Viktor Kozlov
9. Sandis Ozolinsh
8. Ray Whitney
7. Mike Colman
6. Jeff Odgers
5. Jeff Madill
4. J.F. Quintin
3. Gary Emmons
2. Arturs Irbe
1. Dody Wood

SOCCER

TOP 10 WIZARDS

The Kansas City Wizards, one of the charter teams in Major League Soccer, began play in 1996 as the "Wiz." Their name was soon expanded, and the Wizards won the MLS Cup in 2000. Sold in 2006 by Lamar Hunt, the team is looking forward to a fresh start with new owners and a new stadium.

10. Kerry Zavagnin
9. Diego Gutierrez
8. Chris Henderson
7. Miklos Molnar
6. Jimmy Conrad
5. Preki
4. Nick Garcia
3. Chris Klein
2. Mo Johnston
1. Tony Meola

2000 Kansas City Wizards

Courtesy of the Kansas City Wizards

TOP 10 COMETS

The Comets have been around in one form or another since the 1981-82 season. Starting as the Comets of the Major Indoor Soccer League, that team played for 10 years. Brothers Tim and Tracey Leiweke were brought in from St. Louis to run the team. Thanks to the marketing excitement of the Leiweke brothers, before long, Comets games became a happening event, with regular sellouts at Kemper. When the MISL folded after the 1990-91 season, the Attack of the National Professional Soccer League came to town. In July 2001, the NPSL became the new MISL, and the name of Kansas City's team went back to the Comets. Whew!

10. Jamar Beasley
9. Clive Griffiths
8. Alan Mayer
7. Yilmaz Orhan
6. Jan Goosens
5. Casey Barton
4. Dino Delevski
3. Zoran Savic
2. Enzo DiPede
1. Gino Schiraldi

"Where Have You Gone?"

GINO SCHIRALDI

Gino Schiraldi had it all. On a team that was one of the most popular in Kansas City sports history, he was one of its most popular players. So much so that he even received countless invitations to weddings and bar mitzvahs from people he'd never met.

Schiraldi always thought he'd go back to his native Canada after his career as a member of the original Kansas City Comets indoor soccer team during the 1980s ended.

Instead, he parlayed his off-field popularity into several successful businesses. He opened a pizzeria, which lasted about eight years, and then owned a Lamar's Donuts franchise for a decade. Oh, and then there was the Taco Bell and the gas station/convenience store.

As with many parents these days, though, Schiraldi, who was passionate as a player, was working so hard toward the American dream that he often neglected those for whom he was working: his family, a wife and three daughters. In 2001, a year after his wife asked for a divorce, Schiraldi received another wake-up call that led him to a happier, more contented place in his life.

Three weeks before Schiraldi's 42nd birthday, shortly before a scheduled trip to take his daughters on a spring break trip to Colorado, Schiraldi hadn't been feeling right. As a former professional athlete, he was well aware of how his body should feel. This wasn't it. His doctor suggested that he try out this new procedure called body scan imaging. Schiraldi acquiesced.

"My doctor called me back after the test and said he needed to see me right away," Schiraldi says.

The test results showed that the plaque level around Schiraldi's heart was 95. Ideally, it would be 0.

"(The doctor) told me there was no way I was going skiing because I was a walking time bomb," Schiraldi added. "Hearing that was a major blow in my life because I was 42, an athlete, but I was diagnosed with clogged arteries."

So, instead of celebrating his birthday with thoughts of the mountains, Schiraldi was on the operating table for what turned out to be eight bypasses.

"That was a scary time that gave me a different perspective on life," said Schiraldi, who takes medication and keeps tabs on his heart condition — even though he sometimes has a tough time avoiding a good, hot Italian sandwich.

Schiraldi's new outlook on life, along with the divorce, gave him a strong desire to spend more time with his daughters, Gina, Alix and Shelby, and to get back to his other love, soccer.

He has been able to combine the two largely through a soccer club called, not coincidentally, the KC Comets.

The club, which Schiraldi considers "very competitive," includes 17 teams, ranging from U9 to U18. The coaches include Schiraldi, along with other former pros such as Nate Houser, Enzo DiPede, Jamar Beasley and Chris Damico.

"We're giving the players quality coaches early in their careers, which will be helpful later on," said Schiraldi, whose U16 team has won the state title three years in a row. "I'm also trying to help the older kids get a (college) scholarship. We stress to them that education comes first, and then we have fun."

Along the way, Schiraldi's had a chance to coach all three of his daughters: Gina, Alix and Shelby.

"I swore up and down that I'd never coach them, but I love it," said Schiraldi, who's proud that each of his daughters has worn his number 2. "I catch myself sometimes correcting my daughter on the team when I probably don't need to, only to set an example. But they have to earn their playing time, and they understand and respect that.

"I'm so much closer to them now."

Indeed, life's been good for Schiraldi. He's still recognized from his playing days, 1981-91, when the Comets consistently drew large crowds at Kemper Arena. He's proud of the Comets era. Then there are the successful business ventures. But, now, more importantly, Schiraldi's zealous about his job as a father and a youth coach.

"You can do anything you try to do," Schiraldi, says. "In athletics or anything in life, if you fail, sweep the dust off and go again. Just go out and give it a shot.

"You'll hit peaks and valleys. I hit that valley but now I'm enjoying life. Life's too short to not enjoy it."

♦ ♦ ♦ ♦ ♦ ♦ ♦ ♦ ♦ ♦ Section V ♦ ♦ ♦ ♦ ♦ ♦ ♦ ♦ ♦ ♦

AMATEURS

Chapter 12

Stars Align for Jayhawks at Kemper Arena

It was a Rock Chalk "miracle" at Kansas City's Kemper Arena. A bona fide Hollywood ending in America's Heartland for the NCAA's 50th Championship tournament. Led by their Mr. Everything, three-time All-American Danny Manning, the Kansas Jayhawks defied the steepest of odds and upset conference rival Oklahoma, 83-79, winning the 1988 NCAA basketball crown.

"This is something that two months ago was totally unexpected," Kansas coach Larry Brown said after the Jayhawks' title game. "We didn't panic tonight when we got down. We hoped to just get to the last five minutes and take our chances."

"I don't think we've ever played a better game. All the kids played great."

Indeed, Danny and the Miracles, as the team was

Picture courtesy of Rich Clarkson/NCAA Photos

Kansas celebrates its victory at the NCAA Final Four basketball championship held in Kansas City, MO at the Kemper Arena. Kansas defeated Oklahoma 83-79 for the title, April 4, 1988.

aptly called, *were* great. Embracing the underdog role, the unranked Jayhawks surprised the fourth-ranked Sooners in the first half of the title game by setting a furious pace. After running the court step-for-step and matching baskets with each other, the teams were tied after the first 20 minutes.

"When we were 50-50 at halftime, we were shooting close to 70 percent and we were all concerned," Brown said. "We couldn't slow ourselves down."

But Kansas did slow down the tempo and controlled the flow of the game, especially in the last 10 minutes of the second half as they outscored the Sooners 18-11. Manning salted away the win by hitting four free throws in the final 14 seconds.

"It's a great feeling and something we deserved," Manning said following his 31-point, 18-rebound effort against the Sooners. "How do you think this feels, to win a championship and finish your career in Kansas City, in front of the people who've supported you for four years? A lot of people said we were lucky, but what's luck? Luck is when preparation meets opportunity."

An opportunity that, just one month earlier, didn't seem possible. The Jayhawks' road to the school's second national title was long and rocky, filled with disappointing losses, player injuries and suspensions. Highly touted before the season began, Kansas failed to jell as a team and struggled, losing four in a row and falling to 12-8. So poor were the Jayhawks' prospects for the NCAA Tournament at that point that Brown would have been happy to play in the NIT.

Although he had already started making over the team, Brown accelerated his retooling of the Jayhawks at that point. Gone from the mix after 11 games was Archie Marshall, the Jayhawks starting small forward, who suffered the second major knee injury of his career. Marvin Branch (off the team), Otis Livingston and Mike Masucci also were removed from the normal player rotation. Kevin Pritchard became the starting point guard; Chris Piper became a full-time starter, as did guard Jeff Gueldner. Brown wove his players together, tinkered with starting lineups and played the guys who knew that accepting specific roles on the team would result in winning.

The one constant throughout Brown's retooling efforts was Manning.

"It was a manic depressive season," Pritchard said of the 1987-88 season. "We were good, we were bad, we were good, and we were bad. We didn't know which team would show up for games. The team really had a transformation. We went from one team at the beginning of the season to about three or four in the middle, until our final, starting team at the end."

"We got beat by K-State at home to break our long home court winning streak, and we figured we were going to hear it really bad from Coach Brown," said Piper, KU's hometown forward, of the Jayhawks' championship season. "'Hey, guys,' Coach Brown said instead, 'I see us turning the corner. You guys played hard, played great defense. They just hit shots. We're getting better.' And then we got beat by Oklahoma at home again, and the crowd's booing us and stuff. And instead, he says 'No, you guys are getting better.'

"Then we went down to Missouri and beat them, and we had Duke beat here (Lawrence), but lost that in overtime. By then the team really felt like it was a good team. The record didn't show it, but we felt like we could play with anybody."

Brown's coaching, the revamped lineups and, of course, Manning, helped the Jayhawks turn the season around. Kansas won nine of its last 12 games, finished with a 21-11 record and received an at-large bid to the NCAA Tournament.

"The funny thing about 1988 is when we were talking about going to the tournament, it was more like, 'Okay, we've got this tournament. Let's hopefully have a good chance of winning it.'" Pritchard said of KU's attitude before the NCAA Tournament started. "For me, it was more of just wanting to play well versus 'Boy, we really need to win this thing.' We had the attitude of just playing, and then see(ing) what happens. Because of that, I think there weren't the expectations on ourselves that some teams have."

The Jayhawks' road to the Final Four was not going to be easy. Following a relatively easy win against Xavier in the first round, KU almost stumbled against Murray State, but held on for a tight, thrilling 61-58 victory. After they defeated Vanderbilt in the third round, Kansas State, one of the three teams to defeat the Jayhawks at home during the regular season, was waiting for them in the Midwest Regional championship game at Pontiac, Michigan. The Wildcats also had defeated KU soundly in the Big 8 Tournament, 69-54.

"We just kind of really came together as a team, and we knew that if we played well, we could beat anybody," Piper said of KU's tournament run. "We had a guy like Danny on the team that could put us on his back and carry us. It also was unique because in '88 we ended up playing on the road to the Final Four, and once we got there, (there were) teams that we had played before. We played K-State, Duke and Oklahoma, and we knew we could play with those teams."

"Before the K-State game for the Midwest Regional championship, Coach Brown said, 'Let's go out and have some fun. Let's play like we've been playing.' We knew each other so well by then that it was just a matter of who could stop our strengths and who could maximize on our weaknesses," Pritchard said. "Because of that, it was a fun game, a back and forth game. We pulled away at the end and won, 71-58."

At the beginning of the season, playing in the Final Four at Kansas City's Kemper Arena seemed a very real possibility for KU. But when the team dropped its fourth in a row in the middle of the season — an eight-point loss to Oklahoma at Allen Fieldhouse — Kansas City and the Final Four, realistically, was nothing more than a hopeless dream. No matter. The Jayhawks had pulled off the unthinkable. They were headed to Kansas City.

Waiting for KU in the national semifinals was Duke, who had won a heart-stopping overtime game against the Jayhawks in Lawrence.

"I think the most important thing before we played Duke in the Final Four was that we didn't feel pressure," Pritchard said. "We weren't worried about, 'Oh my gosh, if we don't win ...' We just went out and played. Because of that, I think it gave us an advantage over everybody else. That team didn't get tight."

Nerves definitely weren't a problem for Kansas, but Duke wasn't as lucky. KU steamrolled the Blue Devils at the beginning of the game, racing to a 14-0 lead, and with 10:54 left in the first half, led 24-6.

"All great teams make runs at you and they made theirs," Manning said after the Jayhawks won, 66-59. "The same thing happened in Lawrence (when KU played Duke earlier in the year), and we lost the lead and lost the game."

He added: "This is like a dream season. Hopefully, the dream will last a little bit longer."

"The fact that we thought we could win this game was something we talked about beforehand," Brown said after the Duke win. "It was a feeling we had all last week."

The only obstacle left between Kansas and its second national championship was the Oklahoma Sooners, who boasted a 35-3 record coming into the title game. The Sooners also were a team that had beaten the Jayhawks twice that season. But the knowledge they gained from their previous losses to OU was invaluable.

"(Oklahoma coach) Billy Tubbs never liked coming to Kansas City for the Big Eight Tournament," said KU announcer Bob Davis. "Then, for the Final Four, a great moment for him and his team, they have to play the Jayhawks in Kansas City. Maybe that's how it was supposed to be."

After the furious pace of the first half, Kansas slowed the tempo and remained even with the Sooners for most of the second half. Only once, when Kansas fell behind 65-60, did it appear OU would take control of the contest. But KU rallied, and when Piper hit a baseline jumper with 7:16 left, the Jayhawks took the lead, 71-69. After OU tied the score, Kansas scored six straight points. Piper's jumper with 1 second left on the shot clock and 3:05 remaining in the game gave Kansas a 77-71 advantage. A big free throw by Scooter Barry and four final charity tosses by Manning closed out the final 16 seconds of the game—Kansas jumped and waltzed and shouted around Kemper Arena's court in celebration of the 83-79 win.

"I have no regrets about the way my team played," said Tubbs. "Our guys gave a great effort and we played pretty well. I just felt that Kansas had an exceptional game; a heck of a game. ... There are a lot of plays that we would like to replay, but I never missed a lot of sleep over that championship game."

On the other side, Larry Brown had cemented his place among the game's greatest coaches and Danny Manning, the Tournament's Most Outstanding Player, had finished his career at Kansas as — undisputed and undeniable — the best college player in the country. And the unknown supporting cast, unfairly labeled "The Miracles," were crowned the best team in college basketball for 1988.

"The way Danny played in that game was phenomenal," said Davis. "But again, he made the people around him play better. Even taking away his game statistics of 31 points and 18 rebounds, the other guys shot close to 71 percent from the field. They really hit some big shots. ... There were some plays that were very crucial for the Jayhawks in that game."

When 30,000 adoring fans gathered at KU's Memorial Stadium to celebrate the Jayhawks championship, Brown spoke from his heart.

"I've always wondered what this would be like," he said to the cheering crowd. "It was unbelievable. You get a sense of pride when you coach at Kansas because of what Phog (Allen) did and what all the other players and coaches have done, and when you are recognized like that, it's going to take a while for it to sink in."

Kansas forward Danny Manning (25) and Oklahoma center Stacey King (33) during the NCAA Final Four basketball championship held in Kansas City, MO at the Kemper Arena. Kansas defeated Oklahoma 86-78 for the title April 4, 1988.

Chapter 13

KU Players and Coaches

TOP 10 JAYHAWKS

10. *Steve Renko, Baseball-Basketball-Football, 1963-65*

A native of Kansas City, Kansas, Steve Renko was the last three-sport letter winner at KU. He excelled in football and baseball, and spent one season on the Jayhawk basketball team. The Jayhawks' starting quarterback in 1963 and 1964, Renko led KU in passing during his junior year with 505 yards and three touchdowns. As a pitcher, Renko compiled an 8-3 record, 2.60 ERA and struck out 112 opposing hitters in two seasons for KU. Renko, whom the New York Mets selected in the 24th round in the 1965 baseball draft, debuted with the Montreal Expos in 1969. After playing for seven different teams during his 15-year career—the last season with the Royals—he finished his major-league career with 134 wins and 1,455 strikeouts. He joined the Royals organization in 2006 as a pitching coach.

9. *Paul Pierce, Basketball, 1995-98*

While his slashing, athletic style on the court thrilled KU fans for three seasons, Paul Pierce was more than just a scoring threat. He was an all-around player and true star. The Jayhawks' seventh-leading all-time scorer, Pierce finished with 1,768 points for KU and was a consensus first-team All American in 1998. The MVP of the Big 12 tournament in 1997 and 1998, Pierce also pulled in 676 rebounds during his career. The 10th selection overall in the 1998

NBA draft by the Boston Celtics, Pierce has enjoyed a stellar pro career as well.

8. *Clyde Lovellette, Basketball, 1950-52*

The most dominating player in the country during his time at Kansas, Clyde Lovellette led the Big Seven conference in scoring all three years he played (1950-52), was a three-time All-American, and led KU to the 1952 NCAA title when he scored 33 points and grabbed 17 rebounds in the championship game against St. John's. Lovellette has the distinction of being the only player to lead the nation in scoring and win a national championship in the same season. Also, one of only four players to play on an NCAA, Olympic and NBA championship team, Lovellette scored 1,888 points for the Jayhawks — 24.5 points-per-game. Following his KU career, Lovellette played in the NBA for 14 years. He was enshrined in the Basketball Hall of Fame in 1988.

7. *John Riggins, Football, 1968-70*

He smashed through defensive lines for three seasons at KU, running the ball with the force of a sledgehammer. John Riggins, hailing from tiny Centralia, Kansas, was the Jayhawks' top rusher three years in a row. Known as Riggo and "The Diesel," Riggins finished his career at KU with 2,659 rushing yards. His best season was 1970, when he ran for 1,131 yards (fourth-best for a season at KU) and 14 touchdowns. He also won Big Eight all-conference honors twice. Riggins, who spent 14 years in the NFL, was the MVP of Super Bowl XVII. He was elected to the Pro Football Hall of Fame in 1992.

6. *Kirk Hinrich, Basketball, 1999-2003*

A familiar sight in Allen Fieldhouse for four seasons was a racing Kirk Hinrich, running full-tilt from one end of the floor to the other to either drive to the basket, pass for an easy goal or stop and pop a three-pointer for the Jayhawks. A third team All-American in 2003, Hinrich led the Jayhawks to back-to-back Final Fours in 2002 and 2003. He was also a first-team All-Big 12 selection in '03. Hinrich finished his career at KU with 1,753 points and was the seventh overall pick by the Chicago Bulls in the 2003 NBA draft.

University of Kansas basketball players Wayne Simien, Kirk Hinrich and Drew Gooden (l-r) with Roy Williams, as University of Kansas head basketball coach, during Final Four game, Atlanta.

Courtesy of AP Graphics

5. Dr. James Naismith, Basketball Coach, 1898-1907

He was the first basketball coach at the University of Kansas, and the only one in the program's history with a losing record. But, let's face it — if it weren't for Dr. James Naismith there wouldn't be basketball at Kansas, or anywhere else for that matter. Naismith, who invented the game of basketball at Springfield College in 1891, changed the sporting world forever. Interestingly, Naismith is given credit for inventing the football helmet, also. The National Basketball Hall of Fame, where he was elected in 1959, is named for him.

4. Dr. Phog Allen, Basketball Coach, 1907-09, 1919-56

Dr. Forrest "Phog" Allen is remembered as the "Father of Basketball Coaching," but to the University of Kansas, he *was* basketball. The highly innovative and at times gregarious "Doc" Allen coached at KU for 39 years, posting a record of 591 wins against 219 losses. His many coaching accomplishments for KU include winning or sharing 24 conference titles, spearheading the drive to include basketball in the Olympics, winning the 1952 NCAA championship, helping to found the National Association of Basketball Coaches (which is headquartered in Overland Park), and coaching 14 All-Americans. Phog Allen was elected to the Naismith Memorial Basketball Hall of Fame in 1959.

3. Gale Sayers, Football, 1962-64

Hailed as the "Kansas Comet," Gale Sayers' dazzling runs, improbable cuts and surprising speed made him one of the greatest running backs in the history of football. A two-time All-American at Kansas, Sayers' KU career was filled with spectacular plays, including a 99-yard run against Nebraska in 1963 and a 96-yard kickoff return against Oklahoma in 1964.

Sayers concluded his time at KU with 2,675 rushing yards and went on to a spectacular, although brief, career with the Chicago Bears in the NFL. He was inducted into both the College Football Hall of Fame and the Pro Football Hall of Fame in 1977. At the age of 34, Sayers was the youngest inductee ever in the Pro Football Hall of Fame.

2. *Danny Manning, Basketball, 1984-88*

The Jayhawks' Mr. Everything, two-time All-American Danny Manning left KU as the school's all-time leading scorer with 2,951 points — he also led KU to an improbable national title in 1988. In Kansas' win over Oklahoma in the NCAA championship game, Manning had 31 points, 18 rebounds, 5 steals and 2 blocked shots. He was named the Most Outstanding Player in the tournament. Winner of the Naismith Player of the Year and John Wooden Player of the Year awards in 1988, Manning went on to play 15 seasons in the NBA with seven different teams.

1. *Wilt Chamberlain, Basketball, 1957-58*

The single-greatest overall force to ever step on the court for the Jayhawks, Wilt Chamberlain dominated the game unlike any player before or since. A two-time unanimous First Team All-American, Chamberlain scored 1,433 career points and grabbed 877 rebounds in just 48 games. Called "Wilt the Stilt" and the "Big Dipper," Chamberlain scored 52 points against Northwestern in 1957 and grabbed 36 rebounds against Iowa in 1958 — both remain school

records. He was the NCAA Tournament's Most Outstanding Player in 1957 when KU lost the championship game to North Carolina in triple overtime. Chamberlain

Picture courtesy of AP Photo

Wilt Chamberlain poses with Dick Harp, in his first year as head coach for Kansas, on March 21, 1957.

left after his junior year to play for the Harlem Globetrotters. Then, during his 14-year NBA career, Chamberlain led the league in scoring seven times and rebounding 11 times. He was enshrined in the Basketball Hall of Fame in 1979.

"Where Have You Gone?"

MAURICE KING

What a difference a season makes. The Kansas Jayhawks began the 2004-05 season as the Associated Press' No. 1 team. The next year, the Jayhawks struggled to get top-25 votes.

The more unusual of those two positions for KU is being the top team in preseason. In fact, before '04-05, the Jayhawks hadn't been the Associated Press' preseason No. 1 basketball team since the 1956-57 season.

That team, which eventually lost in the national championship game to North Carolina in triple overtime, was led by the likes of Wilt Chamberlain and a guard from Kansas City, Maurice King.

"Sometimes that (preseason) rating can be the kiss of death," said King, who's retired in the Kansas City area. "The rating wasn't pressure for us. We had a pretty good surrounding cast for Wilt. We had some guys who could play basketball. But certainly, Wilt made us a pretty doggone good basketball team."

King, who went to high school at R.T. Coles, was used at both forward and guard during his three varsity seasons, 1954-57, at Kansas. He averaged 14 points per game as a junior and then 9.7 points per game during his senior year.

King went on to enjoy a pro career in the NBA and the American Basketball League with teams including the Boston Celtics, Chicago Zephyrs and Kansas City Steers. But he has spent the majority of his life in the Kansas City area, working toward helping people.

He taught physical education, health and social studies for one year and then became a guidance counselor for one year at the former Northwest Junior High School in Kansas City, Kan. During those two years, he also worked part-time at Hallmark Cards.

In 1968, King accepted a full-time job at Hallmark, where he worked in various positions ranging from human resources to area production manager to recruiting manager of manufacturing until retiring in 1991.

"I managed a training center that Hallmark established in 1968 with its purpose to make job-ready inner-city people who might not have graduated from high school or had some minor difficulties with the law or other issues that might not have made them acceptable in the regular job market," King said of the first full-time job he held with Hallmark before moving up in the company.

Since retiring, King has worked at an alternative school in the KCMO School District and as a manufacturing consultant. In recent years he has worked with youth in group homes and has spent time on the golf course as a golfer's assistant ... when he's not playing, of course.

"I've kind of been picking and choosing what I've done since retiring," King said.

King's appreciation for and kindness toward people possibly can be traced back to his days at Kansas. As a sophomore, King was the first African-American starter in the Big Seven. That distinction — and the 1950's social repercussions that followed — isn't something many players could handle, especially on road trips to places such as Dallas, Houston and Oklahoma City.

King, however, did.

"Our coaches and players had to go through quite a bit with me on that team because they hadn't had to deal with it before," he said. "My junior year, we took a road trip to Texas to play SMU and Rice. ... When they tried to register us as a team at the hotel in Dallas, management came out and said I couldn't stay there. I ended up staying on the SMU campus with the SMU basketball players. When we went to Houston, the same thing happened.

"That whole trip was a pretty bad situation."

Toward the end of the next season, KU again made the trip to Dallas. This time for the Midwest Region of the NCAA Tournament. And, this time, with national star Chamberlain.

"Since I already had my situation there, I explained everything to Wilt," said King. "They took us to a motel outside Dallas that was brand new and had not opened to the public. The whole team stayed there. That came about because there had been some discussions about my experiences and they didn't want to create a situation with a high-profile player like Wilt in Dallas."

Of course, KU won those two games and the national semifinal game in Kansas City before facing North Carolina, the No. 1 team in the country.

Even though the Jayhawks lost to the top-ranked Tar Heels, 54-53, it's been a hard game for King to swallow.

"That's not a game I like to remember, but people bring it up every year," he said. "I was called for the last foul of the game (with six seconds left), even though I didn't touch (Joe Quigg), and the film shows I didn't. We were up by one and he hit both shots.

"After the game, we went back to KU where they had planned a party for us. Louis Armstrong was entertaining in the main ballroom of the student union, so we all got to meet Armstrong and then addressed the students. But I certainly wasn't in very good spirits after the game.

"Had we been able to make our free throws, our mood would've been different after the game and we would be talking a different story right now."

Chapter 14

MU Players and Coaches

TOP 10 TIGERS

10. *Justin Smith, Football, 1998-2000*

Justin Smith was confident that he'd be a relatively high NFL draft pick if he skipped his senior year of college. After all, the 6-4, 267-pound Tiger defensive end had compiled a then-school record 22.5 sacks, 11 of which came during his junior year, and he was the first true freshman to start every game for Missouri since 1986. Before being the fourth overall pick by the Cincinnati Bengals in the 2001 draft, Smith was an All-American selection. Incidentally, Smith recorded three sacks against Kansas City during the 2006 season opener.

9. *Don Faurot, Football, 1923-24 (Player)*
and 1935-42 & 1946-56 (Coach)*

Even though he's not always listed among the legendary college football coaches, Don Faurot was masterful. "He could take his 11 and beat you, then take your 11 and beat his," said long-time *St. Louis Post-Dispatch* writer Bob Broeg. The "father" of the Split-T formation, Faurot led the Tigers to Big Six conference championships in 1941 and '42.

Don Faurot

As importantly, during Faurot's career, the Tigers were 13-4-2 against Kansas. During both stints as a head coach, Faurot also served as Missouri's Athletic Director.

8. *Dan Devine, Football Coach, 1958-70*

Wherever Dan Devine went during his coaching career, he won. That certainly was the case at Missouri, where Devine finished with a 92-38-7 record and wins in major bowl games of that era: Orange, Sugar and Gator. During his 13 seasons at Mizzou, Devine led nine teams to a national top-20 finish. In 1960, Devine's Tigers were on the verge of a national championship, finishing the season undefeated and ranked No. 1. All they had to do was beat Kansas in Columbia. The Jayhawks won, 23-7, but they had to forfeit because of an ineligible player. The damage had been done, though. The Tigers dropped to fifth in the polls and missed out on the national title.

7. *Kareem Rush, Basketball, 2000-02*

Kareem Rush

Kareem Rush kept alive the Kansas City- to-Columbia basketball talent pipeline that has produced stars such as Larry Drew, Jon Sundvold and Anthony Peeler. Rush, with a smooth outside jumper, had a breakout year as a freshman, recording a double-double in 18 straight games (in this case, double-digits in points and rebounds). The season culminated with Rush sharing the Big 12 Freshman of the Year Award. Rush averaged 21.1 points per game the next season, and then, during his junior year, he scored the third-highest number of points in school history, 712, and averaged 19.8 points per contest. Although he played for only three seasons, Rush finished with 1,584 career points at Mizzou before starting his NBA career.

6. *Steve Stipanovich, Basketball, 1980-83*

Steve "Stipo" Stipanovich was the first Tiger to score at least 1,400 points (1,836) and haul in 900 rebounds (984). As the 7-footer that other teams in the Big Eight couldn't stop, Stipanovich helped lead Missouri to four straight conference championships. In 1983, following a season in which Stipo scored 626 points, he was selected as the Big Eight Player of the Year to go along with his All-American selection and Academic All-American selection. The Indiana Pacers selected Stipanovich with the second overall pick in the 1983 draft.

5. Jon Sundvold, Basketball, 1980-83

It seems appropriate that Jon Sundvold and Stipanovich finished next to each other in the voting for this book. After all, the combined efforts of the two helped lead Missouri to a 100-28 record during their four years at the school. Sundvold, who remains one of the most prolific players from the Kansas City area (Blue Springs High School), left Columbia as the second-leading scorer in MU history with 1,597 points and an 85 percent free-throw mark, which still tops the list. He also played more minutes (4,289) than any other player in Tiger history. Sundvold spent nine years in the NBA with Seattle, San Antonio and Miami.

4. Kellen Winslow, Football, 1975-78

Kellen Winslow had played only one season of organized football at East St. Louis High School before the Tigers took a chance on him. The gamble certainly paid off. After playing in only three games during his freshman season, Winslow, a tight end, went on to become an All-Big Eight selection during his junior year and then an All-American the next season. That year, Winslow led the Tigers in receiving with 479 yards and six touchdowns. After college, Winslow spent nine years with the San Diego Chargers, where he caught 541 passes for 6,741 yards. He became a member of the College Football Hall of Fame in 2002.

3. Brad Smith, Football, 2002-05

In a word, quarterback Brad Smith was amazing for the Tigers.

Brad Smith

By the time his senior year ended, Smith had tied or set 69 records at Mizzou. Some of the numbers are staggering: passing yards (8,799), touchdown passes (56), rushing yards (4,289), rushing touchdowns (46), plus he finished three seasons with at least 1,000 rushing and 2,000 passing yards. One game that stands out from Smith's career happened during his sophomore season against Texas Tech when he ran for 291 yards and scored five touchdowns. And, of course, there was the Tigers' 41-24 upset of Nebraska during Smith's sophomore season when he led all rushers with 123 yards. He also scored four touchdowns. His NFL career got off to a good start with the New York Jets.

2. *Anthony Peeler, Basketball, 1989-92*

During his four years at Missouri, Anthony Peeler blossomed into one of the best shooters in the Big Eight. Playing on teams that reached the top spot in the national polls, Peeler hit 116 three-pointers in his career, 55 of which came during his senior year when he shot an impressive 42 percent from behind the three-point arc. That season, he also averaged 23.4 points per game. His most impressive display came against the rival and third-ranked Jayhawks, in Lawrence, on March 8, 1992. That night, in a 97-89 losing effort, Peeler scored 43 points, including 19 in the final 7 minutes, 30 seconds. The Los Angeles Lakers selected Peeler in the first round of the 1992 NBA draft. Since then, he's had a productive pro career with teams including the Lakers, Vancouver, Minnesota, Sacramento and Washington.

1. *Norm Stewart, Basketball, 1954-56 (Player)*
and 1967-99 (Coach)

It's not often that good players go on to good coaching careers. Norm Stewart did both, and did both very well. As a player at Mizzou in the mid-1950s, Stewart scored 1,112 points. During his senior

year, he averaged 24.1 points per game, which is fourth on the Tigers all-time list. Stewart, who played both baseball and basketball professionally, pitched for Missouri's 1954 NCAA championship team.

As a basketball coach, Stewart brought Mizzou out of some ho-hum seasons. Under Stewart, the Tigers won nine Big Eight conference titles, six

Norm Stewart

Big Eight Tournaments, and reached the "Elite Eight" during two of the team's 16 trips to the NCAA Tournament. His colorful personality led to the famous KU chant, "Sit down Norm." Stewart, who beat colon cancer in 1989, was one of the driving forces behind "Coaches vs. Cancer," which has raised more than $25 million for the American Cancer Society.

"Where Have You Gone?"

RENEE KELLY

Renee Kelly is used to the phone calls. So, as usual, she returns the call and politely says that she isn't *that* Renee Kelly.

"You must be looking for the basketball coach," she says in a soft Southern drawl. "I'm a vice-principal at another school, but I'm not the Renee Kelly you're wanting."

The mistake seems understandable. After all, how many educators named Renee Kelly could there be in Augusta, Ga., a town of about 50,000? Well, evidently, two.

"It's crazy sometimes because, since I'm not listed in the (phone) book, she gets my mail and phone calls," said *that* Renee Kelly. "We joke about it quite a bit."

For Missouri fans, there's no mistaking what *that* Renee Kelly — a basketball coach at Augusta's Westside High School — did for women's hoops at Mizzou.

During her career in Columbia, 1983-87, Kelly set the team record in rebounding with 1,098, and per-game averages in scoring and rebounding, at 17.4 and 9.0, respectively. She also finished just seven points shy of the all-time scoring mark with 2,119 points.

Kelly was the Big Eight Player of the Year twice and was selected as the Big Eight's Female Athlete of the Year once.

"I would have to say out of all that, I'm most proud of my rebounds," Kelly said. "It's simply because I always deemed myself as an aggressive player.

"Plus I've always been a very goal-oriented person, and rebounds were high on my list of goals every year."

Kelly stressed goal-setting to her players at Westside High School for nine years. It must've worked. While coaching at the school in her hometown, she helped turn the program from virtually non-existent to a state tournament team for six straight years.

"We went to the sweet sixteen (in 2006) for the first time in the school's history," said Kelly, who also teaches marketing at the school. "The tallest girl I had was 5-foot-8. But I played with them a little bit during practice. I'd elbow them inside to toughen them up. I think it made a difference."

Kelly's also enrolled at Georgia Southern to work on her doctorate in education with a goal of getting out of coaching and teaching, and going into administration.

157

"I want to spend more time with my family," said Kelly, who has two daughters with her husband of ten years, a firefighter and former bodyguard for comedian Eddie Murphy. "It's time to move on and spend time with my kids at their games."

Kelly certainly took basketball as far as she could. After concluding her career at Missouri, Kelly played professionally for four years in Italy and Brazil. This was before the WNBA began play in 1997.

Still, those four years at Mizzou are tough to beat.

"I have so many great memories and great friends from my days at Missouri," she said. "I stay in touch with several of my former teammates and Coach (Joann) Rutherford.

"One thing we laugh about is a trip we took to Long Beach (Calif.) during Christmas break. Coach Rutherford fell asleep on the beach and we put chicken bones around her head. Of course, the seagulls started swarming her. We had to wake her up because it was like a scene from the movie 'The Birds.' Coach didn't think it was funny, but it definitely was one of the funniest things I've ever seen."

It was pretty easy for Rutherford to forgive Kelly and the other Tigers. After all, that was an important time in Mizzou's basketball history, when the Tigers made five-straight NCAA Tournament appearances, 1982-86. They advanced to the second game in 1982 and in 1986, Kelly's junior year.

"The Tournament was the focus for our teams. You had to get to that point," she said. "Coach Rutherford's standards and our expectations were so high that if we didn't at least go to the Tournament, our season wasn't a success."

Kelly and former teammate Joni Davis are the only two Missouri women's players to have their jerseys retired. Both were in Columbia in 2005, when their numbers were raised to the rafters of the new Mizzou Arena.

"The arena is so impressive, I couldn't believe it," said Kelly, who hadn't been to the Mizzou campus since her jersey was first retired in 1994. "I told the team before the game to give me a uniform because I was ready to get back out there. What a place to play!"

Chapter 15

K-State Players and Coaches

TOP 10 WILDCATS

10. *Lon Kruger, Basketball, 1972-74 (Player) & 1986-90 (Coach)*

A Big Eight Sophomore of the Year and two-time Big Eight Player of the Year, Lon Kruger helped lead the Wildcats to back-to-back Big Eight championships in 1972 and '73. In '74, Kruger led the Wildcats with a 17.6 points per game scoring average, which included a 37-point performance against Colorado at the Big Eight Holiday Tournament. Then, during his four years as a head coach at K-State, Kruger led the Wildcats to four straight NCAA Tournament appearances, including the 1988 team that lost to Kansas in the "Elite Eight."

Although best known as a basketball player and coach, Kruger was also a quality baseball pitcher. In fact, the NBA's Atlanta Hawks picked Kruger in the ninth round of the 1974 draft, the same year that the St. Louis Cardinals selected him in the baseball draft.

9. *Bob Boozer, Basketball, 1957-59*

Bob Boozer was one of K-State's first athletic stars. He had the size (6 feet 8, 220 pounds) to bang inside, but the finesse and shooting touch to drain the 20-footers. During his three varsity seasons in Manhattan, Boozer, who averaged 21.9 points and 10.7 rebounds a game, was a three-time All-Conference performer and a two-time All-American. Besides playing on a college team that reached the Final Four, Boozer was a member of the 1960 U.S. gold-medal winning Olympic team in Rome that was inducted into the Olympic Hall of Fame in 1984. Then, after being the first player chosen in the 1960 NBA draft, by the Cincinnati Royals, Boozer ended his career as an important part of the Milwaukee Bucks' 1971 NBA championship team.

8. Rolando Blackman, Basketball, 1978-81

If K-State had an award for player who could do it all and at clutch times, Rolando Blackman would be at the top of the list. Starting 116 of 121 games during his four years, Blackman averaged 15.2 points per game (1,844 overall, good for second on the Wildcats' all-time list). Blackman also was a three-time winner of the Big Eight's Defensive Player of the Year award. In 1980, Blackman, an All-American selection, was a starter for the U.S. Olympic team. The next season, after he was co-winner of the Big Eight's Athlete of the Year award, the Dallas Mavericks picked Blackman in the first round of the NBA draft. He spent 13 seasons in the NBA, mostly with the Mavericks, who retired Blackman's jersey during the 1999-2000 season.

7. Lynn Dickey, Football, 1968-70

After leading Osawatomie High School to an undefeated state championship season in 1966, Lynn Dickey became one of the most prolific passers in Big Eight conference history. During his three varsity seasons at K-State, Dickey threw for more than 6,200 yards and 29 touchdowns. In 1969, when he threw for 2,476 yards, Dickey had four games with more than 375 passing yards. In November of that year, he racked up 439 yards against Colorado in a 45-32 loss. One of Dickey's career highlights, however, came earlier that season when he passed for 380 yards on homecoming, as the 18th-ranked Wildcats knocked off No. 11 Oklahoma, 59-21. Dickey went on to a 15-year NFL career with Houston and Green Bay.

6. Jack Hartman, Basketball Coach, 1970-86

During a 17-season career at Kansas State, Jack Hartman became the winningest coach in school history. His Wildcat teams won nearly 300 games (295), three Big Eight titles, and reached the NCAA Tournament seven times and the NIT once. In 1981, Hartman's Wildcats made an improbable run during the NCAA

Tournament, reaching the West Regional Finals where they lost to North Carolina. Prior to starting his coaching career, Hartman, who played basketball and football at Oklahoma A&M (now Oklahoma State), played one season in the Canadian Football League.

5. *Gary Spani, Football, 1974-77*

The Wildcats were anything but good during Gary Spani's four years as a middle linebacker. In fact, the team won 10 total games in those four seasons, and only one Big Eight game. Spani, a Manhattan native who averaged more than 12 tackles per game in college, was K-State football's first consensus All-American. He finished his career with 543 tackles. In 2002, Spani, who went on to a fantastic career with the Kansas City Chiefs, was inducted into the College Football Hall of Fame.

4. *Tex Winter, Basketball Coach, 1954-68*

Fred "Tex" Winter was one month removed from his own college career at the University of Southern California when he became Jack Gardner's assistant basketball coach at K-State in 1947. Seven years later he took over for Gardner. Today, interchangeable with Gardner as one of the most successful coaches at Kansas State, Winter's teams won eight league championships and made six trips to the NCAA Tournament — and two trips to the Final Four. Also, his .691 (262-117) winning percentage tops the all-time list at K-State. Winter, who's the "father" of the widely-used triangle offense, has nine NBA championship rings as an assistant in Chicago and Los Angeles with players known simply as Michael, Kobe and Shaq.

3. *Jim Colbert, Golf, 1961, 63-64*

Jim Colbert, who went to Kansas City's Bishop Miege High School, spent 17 years on the PGA Tour after an outstanding career at K-State. In 1964, Colbert finished second in the NCAA national tournament. As a pro, including time on the Senior PGA Tour, Colbert has finished in the top-10 129 times, and has made the cut in all but nine events. Colbert, however, has become known over the years by Wildcat fans

Jim Colbert

161

as much for his support of K-State athletics as for what he's accomplished on the links. In 2000, he designed and built Colbert Hills, a PGA-caliber course near Manhattan.

2. *Darren Sproles, Football, 2001-04*

Darren Sproles finished 4th in the Heisman Trophy voting following his 2003 campaign.

Rumor has it, the first time Darren Sproles ran with the football in an organized game, he went 80 yards for a touchdown. He was 9 years old. It was a sign of things to come. By the time he reached the end of his college career, Sproles — who played at Olathe North High School — was arguably one of the best football players in K-State history. During his collegiate career, Sproles set 23 Wildcat records, including most rushing yards in a game (292), a season (1,986) and a career (4,979). He also had 48 career touchdowns and most consecutive 100-yard rushing games (9). The San Diego Chargers drafted Sproles in the fourth round of the 2005 draft.

1. *Bill Snyder, Football Coach, 1989-2005*

There's no denying the remarkable job Bill Snyder did as the head football coach at K-State. He took one of college football's worst situations and turned it into one of the best. Despite going 1-10 during his first season ('89), by 1991 Snyder was able to take the Wildcats to their first winning season since 1982. Two years later, in 1993, the Snyder-led Wildcats started a streak of 11 consecutive bowl appearances that culminated with the January 2004 Fiesta Bowl. During his 17-year tenure, Snyder won more games

Bill Snyder

than the program won in its previous 47 years before his arrival. Toward the end of the 2005 season, Snyder announced his retirement.

"Where Have You Gone?"

MACK HERRON

There's a certain tone in Mack Herron's voice. Part confidence. Part thankfulness. But it's the triumphant part that speaks the loudest. As it should.

Mack Herron, a star running back at Kansas State during 1968-69 at only 5-feet-5 and 170 pounds, has his life turned in the right direction after years of drug use, which helped land him in prison for five years.

"Prison taught me to have more patience and dig deep down in myself to make a difference," says Herron, who had a promising football career ahead of him before drugs got in the way.

His main mission today is researching and working with gangs through a program at the University of Illinois-Chicago.

Whether because of his size or in spite of it, Herron excelled on the football field at everything from catching passes to returning kicks to running out of the backfield.

He finished his career at K-State with 3,150 total yards and 31 touchdowns. By the end of Herron's senior season of 1969, he led the Wildcats in receiving (652 yards), touchdowns (21) and scoring (126 points). He also was a first-team All-Big Eight selection.

Herron was one of the key players who helped turn around the Wildcat program. In 1968 and '69, K-State garnered four and five wins, respectively. The Wildcats hadn't won four games in a season since 1955.

"The big challenge for our team when I got there was turning the program around," said Herron, who started his college career at Hutchinson Community College. "If fans remember me, I just hope they remember what I did on the football field and that I was a part of turning things around."

Professionally, Herron played briefly in the Canadian Football League with Winnipeg before a three-year stint in the NFL with New England and Atlanta during 1973-75. While with the Patriots in 1974, he broke Gayle Sayers' NFL record of combined offense in a season with 2,444. Stardom was on the horizon.

All the while, though, Herron was getting sucked up by the lifestyle afforded by being a pro football player.

"Let's just say that being a pro athlete has some perks," Herron said. "I grew up on the west side of Chicago and all of a sudden I'm in the NFL around money and fame."

And drugs. Herron was disciplined for using marijuana in the CFL. That rap stuck with him in the NFL.

"I loved the game, but once you get one of those asterisks by your name for smoking marijuana, they weren't willing to pay," Herron said. "Even after I served my probation, when we went to contract negotiations, (the Patriots) said I shouldn't be in the NFL. That hurt."

By 1976, he was out of football, largely on his own accord. A few years later, in 1984, Herron was sent to federal prison for five years for drug possession and distribution.

"When you're doing drugs, you don't think about anyone else but yourself," he said. "I got selfish and forgot about what I was supposed to be doing in this world. Prison gave me a chance to think about a lot of things."

Herron started praying for help.

"Man can do a lot of things, but if you want to change, you have to change from your very soul," said Herron, who has lived in Chicago since getting out of prison in 1989. "I realized I was thankful for this life God created, thankful for my mother and father, and I wanted to do some good."

So today, in addition to studying at the University of Illinois-Chicago, Herron is tutoring kids through a church, using the wrong turns he's taken in his life and showing what he could have done differently. He's also helping coach a football team of 7- to 12-year olds.

"I feel like the way God created me, he wants me to do better. He's giving me a chance to give something back," Herron says. "He didn't create me to do drugs or to sell drugs and put people in misery. I found a higher calling and a purpose and that's what I'm doing now."

Herron paused and then added: "We have to make a decision every day to do right or do wrong. I have my priorities in order now. Hopefully I can keep on going like this."

Chapter 16

High School Moments and Players

TOP 10 HIGH SCHOOL MOMENTS

10. *Wyandotte Wins 10 Basketball State Championships*

Under coach Walt Shublom, Wyandotte High School dominated the Kansas state basketball tournament from 1955 to '69. During that stretch, the Bulldogs won 10 championships and finished in second place three times. They reached the championship game 10 straight years, winning five in a row at one point. The program's history is part of a display at the Naismith Basketball Hall of Fame.

9. *Basketball — Central vs. Raytown, Double-Overtime, March 4, 1995*

In front of a packed house at Municipal Auditorium, with a reported 800 people turned away at the door, Central's Derek Hood hit a three-pointer at the end of regulation of the Missouri 4A boys basketball quarterfinal match and sent the game into overtime. Hood, who finished with a career-high 33 points, scored all six of Central's points in the first overtime. JoVonn Jefferson hit what turned out to be the game winner in the second OT. Central went on to win 80-73.

8. *Basketball — Liberty vs. Lafayette, 1998 State Championship*

The Liberty boys finished their perfect season with a 42-41 win over Rockwood-Lafayette for the Missouri 4A state title at Mizzou's Hearnes Center. The Blue Jays had to score 11 of the game's final 13 points to win the game and finish the season with a 31-0 record.

A LEGEND'S HIGH FIVE
NEIL HARWELL

Neil Harwell, who was the first General Manager of Metro Sports, has been on television in the Kansas City area for more than 20 years. During that time, he's announced high school sports, UMKC basketball and small-college hoops. Currently he's the General Manager of the Royals Sports Television Network.

1. Chiefs win first playoff game ever hosted at Arrowhead Stadium in 1991, 10-6 over the Raiders. Deron Cherry picked off two Todd Marinovich passes. Deron had battled back from a serious knee injury a year earlier to become a starter again at safety. Metro Sports' Chiefs show, "Bump and Run," that Deron and I hosted at Bannister Mall, was a blast that week. Our live audience certainly showed him their appreciation.

2. Regional state playoff basketball game Raytown vs. Central before an overflow crowd at the Muny in 1994. Derek Hood (Central) and Tyronn Lue (Raytown) would both eventually play in the NBA. Raytown's team started five guards, four of them under 6-feet. I can still visualize the 5-10 Cerone Webb (Raytown) checking the 6-8 Hood in the post. That Raytown team remains my favorite high school team to watch over the years.

3. Raytown South vs. Lee's Summit, 1990. Ray South won in 2 OT. Jevon Crudup (Ray South) and Patrick Richey (Lee's Summit) would eventually face off in the Big 8 at Missouri and Kansas, respectively. Deric Cofield of Ray South hit three three-pointers inside the final minute of regulation and sent the game to OT. Hanging over this game was a tragic accident in which Ray South star player and KU signee, Chris Lindley, lost his foot just days earlier. Ray South would go on to win the state title in his honor.

4. UMKC (only 2-17 at the time) beats Valparaiso in OT, at Valparaiso, for the first time, before a sell-out crowd, and ended the Crusaders' 20-game home winning streak. I can still visualize

how excited the UMKC coaching staff (head coach Rich Zvosec and assistants Ken Dempsey and Jason Ivey) was after the game in the locker room. The bad part about this game for me was that our producer/director John Denison (ill with kidney stones) and analyst Paul Splittorff (Big 12 scheduling conflict) weren't on the trip. They had seen all of the losses at Valpo but weren't there to see the Kangaroos finally win.

5. UMKC loses to Chicago State, in 2005, on a buzzer beater at the Muny. UMKC was on an 11-game winning streak, packing them in at Municipal. The Kangaroos appeared to be well on their way to making it 12 in a row, but Chicago State scored six points in the last 1.9 seconds and won the game. The first three-point basket by Chicago State was a "no traveling call (I think he was actually moon-walking), H-O-R-S-E, hook shot" out of the corner that dropped in and tied the game. The game winner was an "intercept the in-bound pass, barely touch your hands, all net, 60 foot, jump shot" by Chicago State's Kevin Jones that won the game. I never heard 7,500 fans go that silent before. That shot would eventually be nominated for an ESPN ESPY award for Play of the Year.

7. *Basketball — Rockhurst vs. Liberty, January 4, 2002*

Rockhurst, which had beaten Liberty about a week earlier, blew a 14-point lead in the third quarter at home. Then, in overtime, Rockhurst jumped out to a five-point lead. But Liberty went on an 11-2 run sparked by Josh Duckworth, who sealed the overtime victory with back-to-back shots.

6. *Basketball — Raytown South Coach Bud Lathrop Retires*

Bud Lathrop, the only boys' basketball coach in the history of Raytown South, retired at the end of the 2005-06 season. During his 48 years as a coach — 45 at Raytown South — Lathrop won 954 games, the most by a Missouri boys high school basketball coach.

Bud Lathrop

Courtesy of Bud Lathrop

5. Football — Blue Springs vs. Blue Springs South, November 2, 2001

Blue Springs assembled two drives of more than 90 yards in the second half, and squelched an early lead by rival Blue Springs South. On the first drive, Blue Springs went 99 yards on 11 plays in the third quarter. Then, at the beginning of the fourth period, Blue Springs went 92 yards on 15 plays, and took 8 minutes off the clock for the go-ahead touchdown by running back Andrew Tuggle. Blue Springs 15, Blue Springs South 14.

4. Basketball — Rockhurst vs. Raytown South in State Quarterfinals at Municipal

With star big man Chris Heller on the bench with five fouls, things didn't look good for Rockhurst's quest for a third state basketball championship in 1989 when Raytown South's Rodney Smith hit the go-ahead jumper, 53-52, with less than a minute to play. But after a timeout, with time running down, Matt Ecton passed to Pete Campbell, who put up a 10-foot shot as time expired. The ball went in, and Rockhurst advanced with a 54-53 win. Campbell and Heller led Rockhurst with 16 points each. A week later, Rockhurst indeed won its third basketball championship.

3. Football —Liberty vs. Rockhurst at William Jewell College, 2000

Trailing 17-14 in overtime, Rockhurst quarterback Geoff Brown plowed through the middle on third-and-1, and scampered 15 yards into the end zone for the game-winning touchdown. The game sent Rockhurst to the 2000 Missouri state quarterfinals. Rockhurst eventually won the state title — the program's sixth — and finished the season ranked No. 9 in the USA Today national poll.

2. Football — Kearney Wins Back-to-Back Football Championships, 2002 and 2003

They simply dominated. The Kearney Bulldogs, en route to winning their 25th straight game, dating back to early the previous season, ripped apart Ladue Horton Watkins 43-0 in the Class 4 Missouri state championship game in St. Louis. It also was the 14th straight game that Kearney won by at least 35 points. In December 2002, Kearney beat Eureka 36-22 in the state championship game.

"A Birds-Eye View"

"I was the one lucky enough to hit the shot at the buzzer. That story has been told over and over around the Rockhurst community and beyond since that magical night. I currently teach, coach, and am the assistant athletic director at Rockhurst High School. I have had students come up and tell me how their dad took them to that game. I have had sackers at Hy-Vee who see my Rockhurst Basketball shirt and describe that game — without knowing that I was the guy who hit that shot! I can honestly say that I was not supposed to be the one to shoot that ball. Raytown South did a great job defending our number one option, which was Matt Ecton coming off my screen at the top of the key. He dumped it to me on the roll, and I just let it fly. I remember seeing it go in and then sprinting the length of the floor at Municipal Auditorium, through the exit, under the bleachers, and down the ramp to our locker room. I remember being there by myself for just a few moments, and then my teammates and coaches sprinting down to catch up with me. I was not used to the spotlight, which is probably why I reacted the way I did. In retrospect, I wish I would have stayed on the floor and enjoyed the moment just a bit longer.

"Thank you for including my finest moment with all of these other remarkable games. I don't know that I deserve your nomination, but I appreciate it. Those were good times!"

**— Pete Campbell,
Rockhurst High School, Class of 1989**

Rockhurst Senior forward Pete Campbell smoothly scores against Shawnee Mission West in a 71-54 victory.

Courtesy of Rockhurst High School

1. *Football — Blue Springs, Park Hill, Harrisonville and Kearney Sweep 2003 Missouri State Football Championships*

What a Saturday it was in early December 2003, when the four Kansas City area schools at the Missouri state football championships won each division, beating teams from St. Louis. Things weren't too bad on the Kansas side, either. Olathe North and Blue Valley each won their state championship games, giving Kansas City six football state championships in 2003. (Incidentally, the schools won by a combined score of 215-54.) The area had a chance to get a seventh win, but Centralia beat Lawson in Missouri Class 2.

TOP 10 HIGH SCHOOL ATHLETES

10. *Lucius Allen*, Wyandotte
 9. *The Rush Brothers — JaRon* (Pembroke Hill),
    Kareem (Pembroke Hill) and *Brandon* (Mount Zion, N.C.)
 8. *Jon Koncak*, Center
 7. *Tony Temple*, Rockhurst
 6. *Maurice Greene*, Schlagle
 5. *Anthony Peeler*, Paseo
 4. *Frank White*, Lincoln
 3. *Darren Sproles*, Olathe North
 2. *Albert Pujols*, Fort Osage
 1. *David Cone*, Rockhurst

"Where Have You Gone?"

JON KONCAK

So this is what it means to be both lucky *and* good.

Sure, former Center High School standout Jon Koncak had talent, and being 7-feet tall didn't hurt. But throughout his career, Koncak had a knack for being in the right place at the right time.

Surprising even to him, he was a member of the USA's 1984 gold-medal Olympic team. The next year he was picked fifth overall by the Atlanta Hawks in the NBA draft.

But Koncak, whose competitive basketball career began at the age of 15 when he was discovered by an AAU coach while shooting in the St. Thomas Moore Catholic Church, proved to the basketball world in 1989 that he, indeed, had some luck on his side.

The world champion Detroit Pistons were desperate for help inside after Minnesota picked Rick Mahorn in the expansion draft. The Pistons started courting Koncak, who averaged 6.2 points and 6.1 rebounds per game in his first four years with the Hawks.

A few weeks later, the signing deadline looming, the Hawks matched the Pistons' offer and stunned the basketball world when they signed Koncak to a six-year, $13 million deal.

"I signed on September 15 and got paid more money in the next six weeks than I had in the previous four years," Koncak said from his home near Atlanta. "For 1989 standards, the money was mind-boggling."

Say what you want about the contract that made Koncak one of the highest-paid NBA players, even higher than Michael Jordan. Chances are, Koncak's heard it all before. How he didn't deserve the money. The nicknames, such as Jon Kontract. And, even the one about how he helped raise ticket prices. Hey, he didn't make the offer, he just signed the deal.

"If I had a nickel for every negative comment, I would've made more than 13 million," Koncak said. "If you think there was pressure of being a top-five pick, imagine the pressure of being one of the highest paid players in all of sports."

Koncak says the Atlanta fans were happy that he re-signed. Well, at least until he missed his first shot during a preseason game.

"The bar was set so high that there was no way to succeed," said Koncak. "That was a tough time. At least my coaches and teammates knew I was there to do whatever was needed. When I had those sleepless nights when I was getting booed, I knew the guys wanted me on the team."

In the spring of 1995, Koncak contemplated retiring. The Hawks weren't going to re-sign him. He was 32. His knees were bothering him. Instead, Koncak signed with the Orlando Magic, where he spent one final year that included a run to the Eastern Conference finals.

The next year, Koncak and his family basically fell off the earth.

"Well, we moved to Jackson Hole, Wyoming, which is like falling off the face of the earth," Koncak joked of the place where he lived for seven years and owned a horse farm. "Each year that went by, because we were so isolated, I felt like I had never played basketball before. But I still have the T-shirts and shorts, so I guess I played sometime.

"I wanted to have a normal life with my kids, which we did in a beautiful place."

After going through a divorce in 2004, Koncak moved back to the Atlanta area.

"My day consists of going to the gym, doing some paperwork and then seeing my kids every three or four weekends," he said. "I'm about 20 pounds lighter than when I played because I love focusing on diet and fitness."

Koncak never became the dominant big man that many thought he would, but he was a player who gave his all on the court. Even if he didn't have 20-point, 20-rebound performances every game, if fans wanted to see a 7-foot, 250-pound guy diving after loose balls or swatting shots, Koncak was the man.

"From shooting around a few years earlier in the church gym to reaching the NBA, it was a quantum leap," he said. "Sometimes opportunities are right there and you have to grab them."

THE GOOD, THE UGLY
and
THE AWE-INSPIRING

Chapter 17

Biggest Sports Busts

The most obvious of the biggest sports busts — as someone pointed out in a brainstorming session for this book — would have to be Morganna "The Kissing Bandit." However, for some unknown reason, she didn't receive enough votes. Instead, the following are your favorites. These are the athletes that, right or wrong, were expected to come to the area and make things happen. As everyone knows, things don't always work out as expected.

Morganna comes running out of the stands to kiss Los Angeles Dodger Wes Parker, July 1, 1970.

Courtesy of AP Photo

10. *Mark Davis* —

Expectation: After an incredible season in 1989 with San Diego, where he saved 44 games and posted a 1.98 ERA en route to winning the N.L. Cy Young Award, the Royals thought Mark Davis would be a piece of the puzzle to help them get back to the postseason. They signed him to a fat $10 million contract over three years.

Actual: Mark Davis earned more than $1 million per save. In 95 games with the Royals, Davis recorded seven saves and a 9-13 record. All has been forgiven (or at least forgotten). In recent years, Davis has been a pitching coach in the Royals organization.

9. *Percy Snow* —

Expectation: The Chiefs' first-round selection in the 1990 NFL draft out of Michigan State, Percy Snow was seen as a great addition to the defensive line that featured the top picks of '88 and '89, Neil Smith and Derrick Thomas.

Actual: Sure, Percy Snow started at inside linebacker during his rookie year as the Chiefs reached the playoffs. Then, during training camp the next season, Snow fractured his ankle while driving a motor scooter. He missed all of the '91 season and never returned to form.

8. *Sylvester Morris* —

Expectation: The Chiefs thought highly enough of Sylvester Morris out of Jackson State that they drafted him in the first round in 2000.

Actual: He didn't disappoint, with 678 receiving yards on 48 catches. He showed great promise before a knee injury that cost him the next two years.

Sylvester Morris has yet to play again in the NFL. Although Morris and the Chiefs parted ways, he caught on with the Tampa Bay Buccaneers in 2004, but injured his knee again.

7. *Ricky Clemons* —

Expectation: As a quick and slick guard, Ricky Clemons was going to be one of the leaders for Quin Snyder's Missouri Tigers.

Actual: Oh, where to start with this saga. Basically, Clemons was allegedly involved in several no-no's on campus, including false imprisonment, third-degree assault and allegations of improper benefits. Clemons is a large reason why the NCAA placed the Mizzou men's basketball program on probation in 2004.

Courtesy of AP Graphics

Ricky Clemons, former University of Missouri basketball player, is released from Boone County Jail, Columbia, Missouri.

6. *Todd Blackledge* —

Expectation: Taken in the first round of a quarterback class in 1983 that included John Elway, Jim Kelly and Dan Marino, Todd Blackledge had the Penn State credentials to be selected ahead of Kelly and Marino. Or something like that.

Actual: Who could forget the October 20, 1985 game, when Blackledge threw a team-record six interceptions against the Los Angeles Rams? Blackledge never turned into the starting star the Chiefs needed and thought they were choosing. Blackledge played in 40 games for Chiefs and threw for 4,510 yards.

5. *Colt Griffin* —

Expectation: The Royals saw one of the best high school pitchers, Colt Griffin, as a raw talent when they made him the ninth overall selection of the 2001 draft. In the minors, his fastball reached 100 mph.

Actual: The baseball draft is one of the biggest crap shoots in American sports. Griffin and the Royals proved that. Griffin struggled in the minor leagues, particularly after shoulder surgery, reaching only Class AA in Wichita, before retiring in 2006. He finished with a 19-25 record and a strikeout-to-walk ratio of 271-278.

4. *Bam Morris* —

Expectation: Veteran Bam Morris was a punishing running back for Pittsburgh and Baltimore.

Actual: Bam Morris also was a punishing running back *to* the Chiefs. In addition to his disappointing numbers in 1998 and '99 (895 yards and 11 touchdowns), Morris had a penchant for illegal substances and trafficking.

3. *Trezelle Jenkins* —

Expectation: The Chiefs drafted the man-sized tackle Trezelle Jenkins — 6-7 and 317 pounds — in the first round of the 1995 NFL draft.

Actual: Never able to adjust to the NFL, Jenkins played in just nine games for the Chiefs from 1995-97. He signed with New Orleans and Minnesota but never appeared in a game for either team.

2. JaRon Rush —

Expectation: Talk about talent. During his senior year of high school, JaRon, the oldest of the three Rush brothers, averaged 32 points and 13.2 rebounds a game, leading Pembroke Hill to its second straight Missouri state basketball title. He had his choice of several colleges with elite basketball programs.

Actual: After a couple solid years at UCLA, Rush declared for the NBA draft following his sophomore season. The NBA passed on him and he's bounced around the ABA and other such leagues since.

1. Juan Gonzalez —

Expectation: During his first 15 seasons in the major leagues, Juan Gonzalez was one of the most feared hitters. He had hit at least 40 home runs five times, and had only three seasons with fewer than 19 homers (including the first two years that he spent time in the majors, playing in a total of 49 games.)

Actual: A calculated risk at 34 years old in 2004, Gonzalez joined the Royals on the heels of the club's nearly- remarkable 2003 season. Mired in injuries and a less-than-perfect attitude, "Juan Gone" played for the Royals in one game short of his age and homered just five times.

Chapter 18

Most Inspirational

10. *Tom Watson Wins the 1977 British Open*

Tom Watson's been at the top of his game too many times to keep count. But if there's possibly one moment that defines his career, most people, including Watson would point to the 1977 British Open. The "Battle at Turnberry." The "duel in the sun."

Watson, who had won the '75 British Open, was in the midst of his first great season in 1977. But, he was going up against *the* best at the time, Jack Nicklaus.

The two faced off in a British Open in 1977 that many people consider to be the best golf tournament ever.

After Watson and Nicklaus each shot 68 and 70 on the first two days, they were paired for play on Saturday. The duel began. The two stars blazed the course. Each man shot a 65 and turned the tournament into a two-man event, heading into Sunday's final round dead even.

Throughout much of Sunday, Watson and Nicklaus matched each other shot for shot. Since they were so far ahead of the field, they were going through a great match play. Nicklaus would go up by two or three strokes, but Watson would storm back and tie it.

As author John Feinstein wrote in the book *Caddy for Life*: "(Watson) knew that he and Nicklaus were experiencing something only a handful of elite athletes ever get to experience: the notion that you are facing the best when he is at his best in a setting that guarantees that the outcome will be a part of your sport's history."

Late in the day, on the 15th, it looked as if Watson might be in trouble, sitting off the green about 60 feet from the cup. He sank it.

Tom Watson
June 6, 2001

Courtesy of AP Graphics

The two legends were tied as they headed for the final three holes. After an unspectacular 16th, Watson birdied the par-5 No. 17. Nicklaus shot a 5. For the first time in the tournament, heading to the final hole of the tournament, Watson held the lead alone.

On the par-4, Watson sat on the green, less than a yard from the hole, in two. Nicklaus also made it to the green in two, but his ball sat more than 30 feet away. As one would expect from a champion, Nicklaus drained his putt. Watson took his typically quick approach and sank his short putt for a 65 on the day and his second British Open title.

Watson won five British Opens in nine years, but none was as dramatic as his "duel in the sun" with Nicklaus.

9. *Satchel Paige Pitches Three Innings for Kansas City A's, 1965*

At first, it was seen as another one of Charlie Finley's publicity stunts, which, of course, it was. Satchel Paige, after all, was in the neighborhood of 60 years old in September 1965. (No one knows Paige's exact age.) Finley had pulled plenty of stunts and used other gimmicks to attract fans before. There were the sheep and shepherd beyond the outfield wall. There were the bright green and gold uniforms. And, of course, there was the mule, "Charlie O." So when Finley signed Paige to pitch, a few years beyond his prime, most people saw it as another publicity stunt to help Paige become the oldest person to appear in the major leagues. Of course, it wouldn't hurt Finley's ticket sales, either.

A funny thing happened, though, that night: the Boston Red Sox couldn't hit Paige. He was probably 59 years old and had not pitched in a major-league game since 1953. Yet, as he pitched the first three innings of the game, it looked almost like the same old Satchel who pitched for the Monarchs 20 years earlier.

As if it weren't enough that Paige threw three shutout innings against the Red Sox, he almost no-hit them. Only one batter, Carl Yastrzemski, got a hit — on a bunt. Yes, Yaz decided he was going to get on base by bunting against the aged Paige.

Either way, it was one of Leroy "Satchel" Paige's (and Finley's) finest hours.

8. *Archie Marshall's Last Game at KU*

Archie Marshall's basketball career at the University of Kansas was over before "Senior Day" at Allen Fieldhouse on March 5, 1988. Truth told, Marshall's basketball playing career was finished during the first half of the '87-88 season when he suffered his second serious knee injury — this one to the left knee. (During the NCAA Tournament in 1986, Marshall tore ligaments in his right knee.)

With a little more than a minute left in the game against Oklahoma State, and the Jayhawks holding a comfortable double-digit lead, KU coach Larry Brown inserted Marshall into the lineup. Marshall, with each leg sporting a large brace around the knee, slowly made his way toward the baseline corner of the court to a standing ovation.

As the Jayhawks passed the ball toward Marshall, Oklahoma State coach Leonard Hamilton told his players to back off and let Marshall shoot. Marshall put up a shot from the corner that missed. A basket would've been a fitting end for one of the key leaders for the Jayhawks that won the national championship that year, but it really didn't matter.

"It was very emotional for anyone who saw that," said former broadcaster Max Falkenstien, "because of what Archie meant to the team and for Leonard Hamilton's gesture. I know I'll never forget that."

7. *Joe McGuff Battles ALS*

Without question, Kansas City is a wonderful town. Particularly a great sports town, period, regardless of the teams' local successes in recent years. But no one's cared about it as much — nor possibly been as influential — as Joe McGuff, the sports reporter and former editor of *The Kansas City Star*.

McGuff came to Kansas City in 1948 after starting his newspaper career at the *Tulsa World*. He didn't think he'd be here the rest of his life.

"I came here not really intending to stay," he said. "Wasn't sure where I was headed next, but it was going to be Chicago...New York...who knows. It was going to be someplace where they had Major League Baseball."

Instead of making that move, McGuff stayed here, and was largely responsible for Major League Baseball coming to Kansas City.

McGuff, along with sports editor Ernie Mehl, worked to bring an expansion team to Kansas City in 1967. (A couple decades later, he was a minority owner of those Royals.)

McGuff, through his "Sporting Comment" columns, helped convince his readers of the city's need to build the Truman Sports Complex and Kemper Arena. When Royals owner Ewing Kauffman felt it was time to put a succession plan into place to keep the Royals in Kansas City after his death, he turned to McGuff for advice and to serve on the Board of Directors.

He was inducted into the writer's wing of the Baseball Hall of Fame in 1985.

After guiding *The Star* to a Pulitzer Prize as the paper's editor, McGuff retired on May 1, 1992, after 43 years (38 in the sports department). Seven years later, doctors diagnosed McGuff with amyotrophic lateral sclerosis — also known as Lou Gehrig's Disease.

As expected, he fought the uncurable disease with the same passion that he fought for Kansas City. Seven years later, on February 4, 2006, Joe McGuff passed away. He was 79.

6. *College Students Help Launch Challenger Division*

In 2005, 20 students participating in the Pryor Legacy Program at William Jewell College came up with a great idea. The following summer, they partnered with the Greater Kansas City YMCA and Kansas City Royals Charities and launched the Kansas City YMCA Challenger Division — Little League Baseball's division that's geared toward children with mental and physical disabilities — and a sports complex in the Northland.

The Challenger Sports Complex fields aren't your typical little-league fields. The two baseball fields, will feature a synthetic turf playing surface that can accommodate wheelchairs and other assistive devices. Down the road, so that more of the estimated 20,000 kids in Kansas City with mental or physical disabilities can participate, fields for other sports such as flag football and soccer will be added to the complex.

"There is a huge need for something like this in Kansas City," said Michelle Ford, the Kansas City YMCA's Vice President of Sports Development. "We want to help as many kids as we can."

The Challenger program is something both awe-inspiring and life-changing. It gives the athletes an opportunity, which they might not have had otherwise, to play America's pastime. And, through a "buddy" program, it gives everyone else a chance to participate, also, by helping the athletes.

And to think, even though the YMCA had an adaptive baseball program in place for kids with autism, the ball for the Challenger Division gained downhill momentum with a bunch of college students. Students who are making a difference in Kansas City.

5. *Leo's Comeback*

The date itself isn't very fresh in Dennis Leonard's mind. May 28. Really, it's better to forget it. But, that day in 1983 cruelly altered the rest of Leonard's career and eventually confirmed to Royals fans just what type of player and person Dennis Leonard was.

Facing Baltimore's Cal Ripken Jr., Leonard went through his regular pitching motion. When he landed, though, his knee gave out. His patella tendon was completely severed.

Over the next three years, Leonard went through four surgeries and extensive rehabilitation. He pitched a few innings during the Royals' World Championship season of 1985 when they beat the St. Louis Cardinals. But he chose to spend most of that World Series rehabilitating in Florida.

Leonard's "World Series" reception came six months later. On the last day of spring training, pitcher Danny Jackson twisted his ankle and was forced to miss a start. Leonard, who was scheduled to begin the season in relief, took Jackson's spot on April 12 against Toronto, the fifth game of the season and second at home.

Courtesy of the Kansas City Royals

"To come back and start in Kansas City on a nationally televised game," Leonard says, "I was just hoping I didn't embarrass myself. I felt that if I could go five good innings, I'd be satisfied."

He went more. In fact, Leonard threw a masterful game, allowing just three hits. One of those hits came in the ninth inning with two outs off the bat of Tony Fernandez. If needed, Dan Quisenberry was ready in the Royals bullpen. He wasn't needed.

Dennis Leonard, Royals Pitcher, 1974-86

Leonard ended the game by striking out former Royal Rance Mulliniks. And he preserved the 1-0 shutout.

"It's kind of weird, but that was my World Series. I never worked that hard between starts in my life, from that game in 1983 to my next start in 1986! If I had any guts, I would've quit after that Toronto game," said Leonard, laughing. "I told myself that it wouldn't get any better than that.

"I want to thank the Kansas City fans. There were about 27,000 people there that day against Toronto. They treated me like I won the seventh game of the World Series. It was a storybook ending to three years of misery."

4. *Amos Otis Helps Boys During Flood*

When Amos Otis joined the Royals in a trade with the New York Mets after the 1969 season, he became an instant hit on the field. Fans realized that he was a special player, unlike anyone they saw during the Royals' inaugural season — even, during 1970, becoming the first Royal to appear in an All-Star Game. But, as time went on, even when Otis added Gold Glove awards in center field and more All-Star appearances, fans weren't completely enamored with him. He rarely signed autographs and he often was aloof with reporters.

Oddly, it was something that Otis did away from the field that helped him become a fan favorite in Kansas City.

On September 12 and 13, 1977, nearly 16 inches of rain dumped on the Kansas City area and 25 people died in one of the worst floods in the city's history. That night, as Otis headed home from the stadium after the rainout, he stopped at the Holiday Inn across the street for a bite to eat and a break from the rain. There were eight boys outside, shivering and soaking wet. They were: Jim Bradley, Richard Brown, Joe Harstead, Vernon Holland, Gary Leslie, Vincent Shelby, Welton Shelby and Johnny Strickland.

Because of the torrential rain, the boys' parents couldn't drive to pick them up. A few of the parents called the hotel in hopes of booking rooms for the boys so they'd have a place to sleep for the night. Since the boys all were minors, the hotel manager wouldn't do it, in spite of the weather. When Otis saw the boys, he also tried to get them a room. Still, no dice. So, Otis loaded them into his car and drove them to his house.

"I fed them, washed their clothes and called all their parents to say that they were safe and with me," Otis remembers.

The boys played cards and talked until about 3:00 a.m., when Otis made everyone go to bed. His wife and kids were out of town, so the boys drew cards to see who would get the mattresses and the beds — the low cards got the box springs. Of course, A.O. slept in his bed.

Word got out, thanks to Jim Hunsucker, a neighbor of one of the boys. He heard what happened and informed *The Kansas City Times*.

"I didn't know if anyone was ever going to know any more about it," said Hunsucker. "I mean, here the guy is — usually he doesn't get much support from the public — and here he goes and does something like this.

"I'm a grandfather and if anybody had done anything like that for my kids or my grandkids ... well, I'd just be in his debt forever. And I just think everyone ought to know about it."

"Everywhere I went (after the article), people were telling me that I was a great person for helping those kids. I would hope someone would've done the same thing for my kids," Otis said. "But to (Royals) fans, I could do no wrong after that. I really think that's what put me on the map for Kansas City fans."

A Fan's View

"I was one of the eight kids that was stranded during the flood that hit Kansas City, and was taken home from the stadium by Amos Otis. It was reported in *The Kansas City Times* in an article, "An Otis Unknown to Many." Until that point, many fans had a dislike for A.O. off the field. After this story came out of how he took the eight of us to his Blue Springs apartment and bought us dinner, the public saw another side of him.

Rich Brown (left) and Chiefs Hall of Famer Willie Lanier

"After he couldn't get us rooms at the Holiday Inn, all eight of us piled into his new white Lincoln Continental and he took us to a Jack in the Box on Noland Road. It was raining really hard when we pulled up to the drive-thru and A.O. had to holler into the speaker so the people inside could hear him. The woman refused us service because she said A.O. was yelling at her (she did not know it was Amos Otis). So, he did the next best thing — he bought us whatever kind of microwave sandwich we wanted at a 7-11.

"The next day, a couple of the kids got dropped off at their houses and A.O. met the parents. My parents did not get to meet him, because when we got to my neighborhood, the roads were closed, and A.O. warned us that he could not swim. He let me out and I caught a Metro bus the rest of the way home.

"Before the following Saturday's home game, Otis had all of us meet in front of the double glass doors at Royals Stadium, and he took us into the clubhouse prior to the game while he got dressed. It was a cool experience.

"I had read a story in *The Star* a couple of years ago about what happened to the kid that (former Chiefs running back) Joe Delaney rescued, and how he turned out. Unfortunately, that young man did not make good choices with his life. I want to let A.O. know that I graduated college, obtained an M.A., became a public school teacher and have been named to "Who's Who among America's Teachers" twice in my career.

"You could say that A.O. and that night in 1977 had a huge, positive impact on my life that I'll never forget as long as I live."

**— Rich Brown is currently a teacher
at Wendell Phillips K-8 School in Kansas City, Missouri**

3. Joe Delaney Drowns Trying to Save Boys

What is it that makes a hero do that which is necessary to become a hero?

Unselfishness. That's the only reason to explain why heroes become heroes. They do some sort of act without regard for personal safety or any of the consequences.

That's the only way to explain why Joe Delaney, a promising NFL running back, who didn't know how to swim, jumped into a Louisiana pond in June 1983 — two years after being selected as the AFC Rookie of the Year for the Chiefs — attempting to save three boys he didn't even know.

Unselfishness.

"One of things that comes to mind immediately was his unselfishness," said Billy Jackson, a former University of Alabama running back, who also was drafted by the Chiefs in 1981. "He was always thinking of others before himself. That was off the field and on it."

As a rookie starter in 1981, Delaney rushed for 1,121 yards, including a 193-yard rushing performance against the then-Houston Oilers. In the strike-shortened 1982 season, seven games short, Delaney still mustered 380 yards.

But then, on June 29, 1983, while relaxing in a park in Monroe, La., Delaney heard the pleas of three boys. Instinctively, he hopped up, ran to the muddy water and jumped in. Instead of trying to get someone else to do it since he couldn't swim, he jumped in, trying to save three strangers who also couldn't swim.

No amount of running ability or quickness or speed or agility mattered at that moment. In some ways, Delaney was successful. He saved one of the boys. However, Delaney and the other two drowned.

A few weeks later, on July 13, 1983, President Ronald Reagan posthumously awarded Delaney the Presidential Citizen's Medal. The next year, the NCAA selected Delaney, who rushed for a school-record 3,047 yards at Northwestern State (La.), as the recipient of the NCAA Award of Valor.

Delaney, who also has been enshrined in the College Football Hall of Fame, did what he felt he had to do. He likely didn't sit there in the park and calculate the reasons for or against going in the water. After all, heroes don't think, they act. Delaney acted. Unselfishly.

As with so many other heroes before and after him, Delaney displayed selflessness that June day that is found only in special people. Like Joe Delaney.

2. *Steve Palermo Walks Again*

Fear. Of things that go bump in the night. Of rejection. Of failure. We're afraid for countless reasons. When it matters, though, courage and the act of heroism come out in some people. It's the only way to explain why a major-league umpire would chase down muggers late one night in Texas.

In early July 1991, umpire Steve Palermo, who is a Leawood resident, was enjoying dinner at Campisi's Egyptian Restaurant with some friends after working a Texas Rangers-California Angels game. Suddenly, the bartender shouted out that two of the waitresses were being mugged outside at gunpoint by four men. Without hesitating, without really debating, Palermo, Terance Mann and restaurant owner Corky Campisi — the best man at Steve and Debbie Palermo's wedding just five months earlier — ran to the aid of the two women.

Three suspects got away, while Palermo, Mann and Campisi chased down the fourth. As they held him down, the other three returned in a car. One of the men fired shots, including one that hit Palermo in the back, causing paralysis from the waist down. Another bullet hit Mann.

**Steve Palermo,
March 28, 1989**

Since that night, Palermo has gone through 15 years of hell, rehabilitating and trying to do what the doctors told him he wouldn't be able to do again — walk. Next to him, every step of the way, has been Debbie.

Today, with the assistance of a leg brace and a cane, Palermo is walking again. He's also busier now than he was during his 15-year career as one of baseball's top umpires. Besides being a sought-after motivational speaker delivering a message of "Never Admit Defeat," Palermo is also involved with several non-profit organizations including the

Steve Palermo Endowment for Spinal Cord Injury Research, Education and Clinical Affairs at KU.

Since 2000, Palermo has been the Supervisor of Umpires for Major League Baseball. It's a chance to stay involved in the game and pass along some of the on-field wisdom he gained. It's also just a little something to give him some extra motivation.

"I'm hoping before I get too old that I can get back out on the field, even if it's just to work one game," Palermo told Metro Sports' Erik Ashel during an interview in May 2004. "And then I can leave on my terms if I want."

Impossible? For some. But with what Steve Palermo's gone through since that early morning in July 1991, anything's achievable.

1. *Buck's Hall of Fame Snub*

In early 2006, the Hall of Fame appointed a special panel of "experts" to vote for former Negro League players and personnel for inclusion into the Hall. In many ways, at least to outsiders, it looked as if this was going to be a special favor to help O'Neil, a former voter on the Veteran's Committee, join the other immortals in Cooperstown.

"We all thought he was shoo-in," said Bob Kendrick, O'Neil's close friend and the Marketing Director for the Negro Leagues Baseball Museum. "Granted, we thought in the realm of possibility that he might not get in, but we didn't really think that would happen. ... The difficult thing for Buck was probably hearing everyone assume that he was going to get in. He tried to help us all understand that it might not happen."

The Hall of Fame announcement — when people realized that Buck fell one or two votes shy of being selected — unleashed an incredible public outcry in Kansas City as well as throughout the country. As exciting as it was that the special committee of so-called experts selected 17 people from the Negro leagues, including former Kansas City Monarchs owner J.L. Wilkinson, for the Hall of Fame, Buck O'Neil's *ex*clusion seemed to make bigger news.

Through it all, Buck just sat back and shrugged off disappointment, as he'd done so often throughout his life.

"He was consoling all of us," Kendrick said. "He taught us a very valuable lesson that day in just how to handle it when things don't go our way. You handle it with selflessness, with dignity. And I think he understood that the Hall of Fame didn't define who he was. Certainly he was disappointed, but when you look back at his life and the adversity he faced, the Hall of Fame pales in comparison.

"He had enough support not only in Kansas City, but as we saw, across the great country, to more than make up for what I still see as a great travesty. ... It was gut-wrenching for many of us, myself included. But, we all can find resolve in how he handled that entire situation."

Topping everything, Buck graciously delivered the acceptance speech at the Hall of Fame induction ceremony in honor of those 17 people who did get selected. That's like getting rejected for the prom, only to have the girl ask you to help her pick out the dress she'll wear with the other guy.

In typical Buck O'Neil fashion, though, in what would turn out to be his last public appearance, he delivered a knock-out speech that didn't show a bit of anger or remorse. Completely classy.

Buck O'Neil

Excerpts from Buck O'Neil's Hall of Fame Speech, July 30, 2006

"This is outstanding. I've been a lot of places, I've done a lot of things that I really liked doing. I hit the home run, I hit the grand slam home run, I hit for the cycle, I've had a hole in one in golf. I've done a lot of things I like doing. I shook hands with President Truman. Oh, man. I [shook hands with another] president and I got to hug his wife Hillary. So I've done a lot of things I like doing, but I'd rather be right here right now representing these people that helped build a bridge across the chasm of prejudice, not just the ones like Charley Pride and me that lead across it. Yeah. This is quite an honor for me. ...

"...Negro league baseball. All you needed was a bus, and we rode in some of the best buses money could buy. Yeah. And a couple of sets

of uniforms. You could have 20 of the best athletes that ever lived, and that's who we are representing here today. It was outstanding. And playing in the Negro leagues, which a lot of you don't know, see, when I first came to the Negro leagues, five percent of major-league ball players were college men because the major leaguers wanted them right out of high school, put them in the minor league, bring them on in. But Negro leagues, 40 percent of Negro leagues, leaguers, were college men. The reason that was, we always spring trained in a black college town and that's who we played in spring training, the black colleges, so when school was out, they came and played baseball. When baseball season was over, they'd go back to teaching, to coaching or to classes. That was Negro league baseball. And I'm proud to have been a Negro league ball player. Yeah, yeah.

"And I tell you what, they always said to me Buck, I know you hate people for what they did to you or what they did to your folks. I said no, man, I never learned to hate.....

"So I want you to light this valley up this afternoon. Martin [Luther King] said 'Agape' is understanding, creative — a redemptive goodwill toward all men. Agape is an overflowing love which seeks nothing in return. And when you reach love on this level, you love all men, not because you like them, not because their ways appeal to you, but you love them because God loved them, and I love Jehovah my God with all my heart, with all my soul and I love every one of you as I love myself.

"Now, I want you to do something for me. I'm going to get off this stage, I think I've done my six minutes. But I want you to do something for me. I want you to hold hands, whoever's next to you, hold a hand, come on, you Hall of Famers, hold hands. All you people out there, hold hands. Everybody hooked up? Everybody hooked up? Well then I tell you what, see, I know my brothers up here, my brothers over there, I see some black brothers of mine and sisters out there. I know they can sing. Can you white folks sing? I want you to sing after me:

"(Singing began) The greatest thing, come on everybody, the greatest thing, in all of my life, is loving you. The greatest thing in all of my life is loving you. The greatest thing in all of my life is loving you. The greatest thing in all my life is loving you. (Singing ended)

"Thank you folks, thank you folks, thank you folks, thank you folks, thank you, thank you, thank you, thank you, thank you, thank you. Now, sit down. Now, sit down. I could talk to you 10 minutes longer but I got to go to the bathroom."

Chapter 19

He Could Charge Admission

Jim Chappell sits at the bar of his restaurant in North Kansas City on a Sunday afternoon. Seeing Chappell sit down in the restaurant that bears his name is a rare occurrence.

If the restaurant were open on Sundays, he wouldn't be sitting here now. No, Jim Chappell is usually walking around, taking customers on tours of Chappell's Restaurant and Sports Museum; or going from table to table, greeting customers and telling a quick story about the Lew Krausse/Charlie Finley photograph on the wall, or one of the three antique stadium seats hanging from the ceiling, or that case of autographed baseballs, or the...

You see, Chappell's is the best of every American sports museum, combined. It's sports' version of the Hard Rock Café. It's the Louvre. It's Grauman's Chinese Theatre. It's one of Kansas City's best kept secrets, at least locally. *Sports Illustrated* selected Chappell's as one of the top-10 sports bars in America. So did the *Chicago Tribune*.

Not to sound like a restaurant critic, but the food is very good. Worth coming back for. But, you don't come to Chappell's for the food, at least not the first time. No, it's for the gazillion or so pieces of sports memorabilia — the hundreds of autographed photos, the rare trinkets from the Kansas City Blues and A's, the boxing gloves Sylvester Stallone wore in *Rocky*, and the helmets hanging from the ceiling, representing nearly every local high school, all the pros and most colleges. Even Colgate is represented.

Jim Chappell's Top 10 Pieces of Sports Memorabilia
(In no particular order)

10. 1935 Notre Dame team autographed football
9. Over 1,000 football helmets hanging from ceiling
8. John Wooden's 1930-31 Purdue All-Indiana trophy
7. Len Dawson's autographed Dallas Texans warm-up jersey
6. Dick Howser's 1985 game-worn autographed jersey
5. Michael Jordan's autographed Olympic jersey
4. 1963 Rawlings Gold Glove award (no name)
3. Two Olympic torches, 1984 and 1996
2. Larry Bird's 1979 NCAA Player of the Year award
1. 1973 Oakland A's World Series trophy

"Joe Montana would come in here with Greg Manusky, who went to Colgate," Chappell said. "To give Manusky a hard time, Montana would say, 'Hey, Jim, where's your Colgate helmet?' Of course, we didn't have one. Finally, one day, Greg asked if he could use my phone. He called Colgate and said, 'This is Manuz. I need a Colgate helmet. Send it to...' and he gave my address. About a week-and-a-half later, the helmet showed up.

"That's how I've gotten a lot of stuff. I've never gone out looking for anything. If something's sent in, I put it up."

That's just one of the stories. There are countless others. Taking a tour of the restaurant with Chappell, you're getting a history lesson from that uncle who always tells the greatest stories at family reunions. You could point to practically any piece of memorabilia in the restaurant and get an anecdote behind it, which leads to another story about another item.

Jim Chappell's Top 10 Pieces
of K.C. Sports Memorabilia
(In no particular order)

10. Kirk Hinrich autographed Bulls jersey and shoes, provided by Kirk's dad who's a regular at Chappell's
9. Enos Slaughter bat autographed by the 1955 Kansas City A's
8. Home plate from Municipal Stadium autographed by '55 A's and several Kansas City Monarchs
7. 1956-67 K.C. A's uniforms
6. Kansas City A's jacket that was given by owner Charlie Finley to "the fisherman's friend" Harold Ensley (Ensley's name is inside the jacket)
5. Al Dark and Hank Bauer autographed game-worn jerseys
4. Len Dawson autographed MVP football
3. Hickey Cup — trophy given to the Blues for being the minor-league team with best opening-day attendance
2. Len Dawson's autographed Dallas Texans warm-up jersey
1. Dick Howser's 1985 game-worn autographed jersey

Very rare Dallas Texan sweatshirt worn by Len Dawson.

195

Chappell's is one of those places where, when you walk in, you could almost picture Hank Bauer and Phil Rizzuto during their days with the Kansas City Blues, sitting in a booth over there having dinner after a game. Or some ink-stained reporter from *The Kansas City Times*, relaxing at the bar with a pipe and a beverage after a long day of covering Tom Pendergast.

Only thing is, Chappell's and its dark, ornate wood and antiquated pieces of memorabilia only make the place *feel* as if it's been here for a half-century. It actually opened in November 1986 as a political and sports bar. After about six months, Chappell dropped the political aspect. But the unique, homey feel has been here since day one.

"I decided I wasn't going to have baby blue walls and fake impressionist pictures above the booths," said Chappell. "I wanted this place, from the day I opened it, to look like I opened it 35 years earlier."

Although it might be a stretch to say Chappell's has become Kansas City's place to *be seen* over the years, it's accurate to say that it's not uncommon to see sports stars here at any given time.

Orlando Cepeda, Dave Winfield, Franco Harris, artist LeRoy Neiman and country singer Vince Gill, just to name a few. Of course, Kansas City's sports celebrities have made it to the restaurant. Chappell says during 1993-94, it was common to see Joe Montana and Marcus Allen having lunch. Hank Bauer, George Brett and Len Dawson have been regulars during the past 20-plus years. Even Chiefs owner Lamar Hunt has been seen giving tours to his guests. Over the years, Chappell's also has hosted reunions for the 1955 Kansas City A's, the 1969 Chiefs and, a few years ago, all of the living Kansas City Monarchs players.

"When I opened, I didn't know anybody outside of North Kansas City would have any idea this place existed," Chappell said. "I never thought that people, especially celebrities, would seek it out."

In spite of the celebrity clientele and rare collectibles and great anecdotes, though, Jim Chappell doesn't hesitate when asked about the best thing in the restaurant.

"My customers," he said as he pulls out a Styrofoam baseball displaying the restaurant's logo. "I've had kids come in here years later and say how they got a baseball from me and they still have it. Even adults have asked me to sign those baseballs for them. That means a lot to me.

"Some people have come in to videotape me saying 'happy birthday' to their dad or whoever. I love doing it because it makes them feel good. Shoot, just because I know I'm nobody, they don't think that. It's nice to be in that position to do something to make them feel good. I can do favors for people and they think it's the biggest thing in the world, when it was really easy for me. I love doing that. I love my customers."

Courtesy of Gregg Riess Photography

**Jim Chappell, owner of
Chappell's Restaurant and Sports Museum.**

AS IF
WE'D FORGET
the
MEDIA

Chapter 20

Birth of Metro Sports

Metro Sports went on the air December 12, 1996 in conjunction with the national launch of CNN*SI*, but the idea began nearly a decade earlier.

"We (American Cablevision) started doing more sports programming in 1986, including high school games, the NAIA basketball tournament, UMKC basketball, the Comets and the Chiefs' 'Bump & Run' Show," said John Denison, who is now the General Manager of Metro Sports. "We started with a Missouri basketball package of a few games, including a game in Carbondale against Southern Illinois."

Denison and Neil Harwell, who usually served as the announcer/host for these early games, drove to Carbondale the day of the game. When they arrived a couple hours before tip-off, their production truck was in the parking lot, idling. The powers-that-be weren't allowing the production crew to hook up the truck.

"(Southern Illinois) said that we didn't have the rights to do the game," said Denison. "We'd already driven seven or eight hours only to find out that we might not be able to do the game."

Nevertheless, the crew frantically set up the equipment as Harwell went inside and worked out a deal to be able to

Courtesy of Metro Sports

Then General Manager, Neil Harwell (left) and host Duke Frye publicity photo promoting launch of Metro Sports on December 12, 1996.

broadcast that night's game. As oftentimes happens in this business, the viewer had no idea of the chaos that transpired minutes before show time. The broadcast went off without a hitch and Denison and Harwell completed their 26-hour day by driving back to Kansas City after the game.

There was one glitch in those Missouri telecasts pre-Metro Sports days, however.

The Tigers played host to Nebraska on a blustery day, complete with ice and snow. On the way to Columbia, the station's uplink truck slid off the road and into a ditch. So, they "borrowed" an uplink truck from another station.

Everything was going smoothly. The game was exciting. Denison was doing his typically great job of directing the telecast, while Harwell, who was actually the cable company's marketing manager, sat nearby in the truck, "where I have absolutely no business being."

"My boss, Jeff Johnston, called and said we weren't on the air," Harwell continued. "They were getting a ton of calls to the switchboard. I went out and found out our uplink had gone down. It was frozen. One of the guys that worked for that other station was at the top of the truck without a coat or any gloves, in a wind chill of about 30 below, trying to fix the uplink. Finally I went back inside the truck and told John that from halftime on, our game wasn't on the air.

"We've joked that the money we lost that day was the equivalent to driving a brand new Jeep Cherokee off a cliff."

Despite some early success with Missouri basketball games, and the popular "Bump & Run" Chiefs show that Harwell co-hosted with Deron Cherry on Wednesday nights — which once included cutting Rich Baldinger's hair on the show — the timing wasn't quite right to pursue a full-fledged all-sports channel.

A few years later, though, two very different men, Dennis Mahon of the Ku Klux Klan and Rev. (now Congressman) Emanuel Cleaver, helped provide the impetus for the birth of Metro Sports.

In the 1980s many cable companies offered what was called "Public Access" channels as part of their franchise agreements with their local governing body. By federal law, there could be no restrictions on the content of public access shows. Free speech at its best! Seeing an opportunity to spread its message of hate, the KKK sent Mahon to Kansas City from Oklahoma to take advantage

Top 10 Kansas City Sports Announcers

10. Paul Splittorff
9. Max Falkenstien
8. Bob Davis
7. Bill Grigsby
6. Len Dawson
5. Mitch Holthus
4. Neil Harwell
3. Fred White
2. Denny Matthews
1. Kevin Harlan

of then-American Cablevision's public access channel. Citing its own concerns, the cable company resisted Mahon's appearance.

A city councilman from Kansas City's fifth district, Rev. Cleaver, sympathized with the cable company's desire to resist the Klan, but a federal judge sided with the Klan (represented by the ACLU). And so, in 1990, a shocking program called "Klansas City" aired on channel 30.

Rev. Cleaver, soon to be elected mayor, convinced the remainder of the City Council that public access requirements should be omitted from the cable franchise. So, in Kansas City, as well as in many other cities, public access studios eventually went dark.

Once the cable company was relieved of its public access obligations, that channel became available for some other type of programming. A team including company president Bob Niles, Carol Rothwell, Jack Nott and John Denison began to explore what kind of local programming might benefit subscribers and use the production staff's abilities. A small core of talented producers had supplemented their work for the cable company by freelancing with outside companies such as ESPN, Fox Sports, PBS, and others, so the selection of sports programming for the cable company was a natural, although the group also explored other ideas, including a Kansas City arts station.

Carol Rothwell, who was American Cablevision/Time Warner's vice president of public affairs and production until 2006, hired Neil Harwell, who had left the company a couple of years earlier, to return as Metro Sports' first General Manager.

Harwell brought in established Kansas City sports personalities Duke Frye and Brad Porter as the first sportscasters. Production was handled by Denison (now General Manager) for the first few months. The company had also cobbled together a production truck in 1987 in order to cover local high school games and produce a Chiefs talk show to air on the cable company's community channel.

With a staff of about a dozen people, a few additional pieces of production equipment and a simple automation system, the former community channel was converted to a sports channel capable of at least one daily talk show and one live game per day.

As can be expected, things weren't always perfect.

"On our first day for the show ("Metro Sports Talk"), we were trying to get a set made," said Denison, "and we were waiting on the main piece, the table, which we thought was going to be really nice. They delivered it an hour before the show, and it looked horrible. It was junk. Of course, we stuck with it for two years, but it looked horrible."

Metro Sports Staff 1996

(Back Row L-R) Paul Boggess, John Denison, Emiel Cleaver, Eddie Dean, Jeff McKee, Randy Miller, Edwin Birch (Front Row) Chris Huwe, Neil Harwell, Carol Rothwell, Duke Frye, Jack Nott, Russ Gardner, Curtis Lorenz.

Metro Sports has grown beyond its early dreams since then. The station now includes more than 35 full-time employees and hires hundreds of free-lancers. And, it's grown from that one make-shift production truck to five production trucks that blanket the Midwest covering professional, college and high school sporting events for Metro Sports and other networks. In 2003, KCTV-5 (Kansas City's CBS affiliate) began out-sourcing its sportscasts to Metro Sports. Rather than have its own three-person sports team and the staff to support them, KCTV hired Metro Sports to provide turnkey sportscasts for their newscasts, as well as produce all sports-related programs. KCTV's sportscasts look like they're coming from the next desk rather than over fiber from a studio miles away.

Time Warner had a unique opportunity, had some production equipment and had the right people with a passion for sports to launch a dream that started 10 years earlier, and has benefited Kansas City sports fans ever since.

The Metro Sports staff shows its spirit, 2006

HIGH FIVE
NAIA MOMENTS

A highlight each March for Metro Sports viewers has been the NAIA men's basketball tournament championship game, which John Denison, Neil Harwell and others started broadcasting on American Cablevision in the late 1980s. "A lot of championship games are snoozers," said Denison. "The NAIA has the best championship games. They almost never have a dud." Denison and Harwell offer the following list of memorable NAIA moments.

1. *Life vs. Georgetown, 2000.* In the late 1990s and early 2000s, Life University, which is mainly a chiropractic school in Atlanta, dominated the tournament. The school's founder and president was a big, boisterous guy named Dr. Sid Williams — he went by Dr. Sid. (He played football at Georgia Tech when they won the national championship in the early '50s.) Life had a star player in that stretch named Jimmie "Snap" Hunter, who went into the NBA. Snap just took over this one tournament. Nobody could stop him. Suddenly, in crunch time of the championship game, Snap went down with an injury. Life traveled with a chiropractic table and what looked like a chiropractic student to give players minor adjustments during the game if needed. When Snap went down, they set up the table next to their bench. But, instead of this student trying to help Snap, Dr. Sid comes rushing out of the stands, announcing that he needs to make the adjustment on the team's star player. Snap went back in the game and he hit the game-winning shot, giving Life its third national title in four years.

2. *Life vs. Mobile, 1999.* That year, Life had the quickest college team we've ever seen, including NCAA teams. Let's put it this way: it's the quickest team that's ever been on Metro Sports. Every guy was under 6-5 and their opponents averaged more than 30 turnovers a game. Life was down by 26 points with 11 minutes left in the game

against Mobile. Life battled back, and in the final seconds, Corey Evans got the ball after a Mobile free throw, wove around defenders to the other end of the court, and let loose of a 20-foot game-winner, landing on his face as the buzzer sounded.

3. *Kris Bruton, Benedict, 1994.* One of the NAIA guys we've enjoyed the most through the years has been Kris Bruton from Benedict College in South Carolina. In 1994, he helped lead Benedict to the quarterfinals. The incredible thing about Bruton was that he could get his shot off against anybody. He was 6-7. He wasn't flashy but he could jump out of the arena. During a 9 a.m. game in '94, he jumped over a guy who was 5-11 — literally jumped over him — and then dunked the ball. A few weeks later, we each were at our houses watching the college slam dunk contest during the NCAA Final Four weekend. They were announcing all these guys from NCAA schools. They came to the last name: "From Benedict College, Kris Bruton." We called each other and immediately said that he was going to win it. Sure enough, Bruton won it when he jumped over a ball rack from about 10 feet out. After being drafted by the Chicago Bulls in '94, Bruton eventually ended up with the Harlem Globetrotters.

4. *Texas Wesleyan vs. Oklahoma City, 2006.* When Ben Hunt decided to leave Australia and go to college in the U.S., he spun a globe and pointed. From that he picked Texas Wesleyan. In 2006, as a 28-year-old senior, Hunt rebounded a missed free throw, with Oklahoma City leading by a point, wove through the defense and hit a three at the buzzer for the 67-65 win.

5. *Science & Arts vs. Oklahoma Baptist, 2002.* The biggest thing about this championship was that it was the first one back in Kansas City after the NAIA spent eight years in Tulsa, Oklahoma. When the tourney came back in '02, we televised every game on Metro Sports, and did a *Total Access* show. It was a ton of work, but definitely a highlight for us.

♦ ♦ ♦

A LEGEND'S HIGH FIVE
LEN DAWSON

A list from Len Dawson could appear in several chapters in this book. A couple of his biggest games as a QB are featured in Chapter 2. He's featured, along with more games, in Chapter 9. Today, many people know Dawson for his work on the Chiefs Football Radio Network and at KMBC (Channel 9), where he started working when he was still playing for the Chiefs....and he's done well, considering he's in the sixth spot in our two "favorite" media lists in this chapter.

1. 1969 Super Bowl
2. 1985 World Series
3. Chiefs 1971 Christmas Day game vs. Miami
4. The 1966 season, which ended with Super Bowl I
5. Kansas winning the '88 NCAA Tournament at Kemper

Top 10 Kansas City Sports Media People

Author's Note: Are you kidding me? Are you kidding me? I have very few arguments with the top-10 lists throughout this book ... except this one. As much as I'm flattered that people voted me at the top, the fact that I'm even in the top 10 almost makes every other list in the book lose credibility — and it proves the idea of global warming and that Elvis might actually be pumping gas in Smyrna, Georgia. Personally, I would have put Joe Posnanski in the top spot and Soren Petro higher than No. 8. I also feel that Dick Kaegel, Bob Dutton, Blair Kerkhoff and Mechelle Voepel should be on this list as well. But then it would have been a top-13 list. So, excluding No. 1, this is a list of media people that could go up against the top 10 in any other market.

10. Harold Ensley
 9. Jack Harry
 8. Soren Petro
 7. Kevin Kietzman
 6. Len Dawson
 5. Joe McGuff
 4. Frank Boal
 3. Dave Stewart
 2. Joe Posnanski
 1. Matt Fulks

A LEGEND'S HIGH FIVE
DAVE STEWART

1. Birth of the Royals in 1969. A classmate of mine's dad was controller for the team so we went to a lot of games. My mom would drop us off at the game, he would drive us home. I remember watching BoSox outfielder Reggie Smith, in his rookie year, absolutely go off. I still have a little piece of notebook paper signed by Lou Piniella, Mike Fiore, Dave Wickersham, Joe Foy and others. We also picked up one of Joe Foy's cigarettes. "You can keep it, kid." We did. It sparked my passion for baseball and the Royals. I always wanted to play right field for the Royals and go to the Baseball Academy. Instead, it led to this life of leisure, getting paid to talk about 'em. Ha!

   Of course, Joe Keough had the first game-winning RBI in Royals history against Minnesota. Then, I think it was in the '71 season, he broke his leg/ankle sliding into home plate — they said you could hear it POP in the upper deck. Anyway, I sent him a get-well card, and he sent me a personalized note back. Needless to say, I was blown away by it.

2. 1985 ALCS in Toronto. Watching Royals win games 6 and 7 at a crappy football stadium. Sneaking into a football suite to keep from sitting in the outdoor press box and freezing to death. Toronto people were extremely nice before Game 6 because the Royals had no chance of winning twice. They turned rude and scary after Game 7. A bunch of drunks knocked down a barrack 'protecting' me during a live shot. I thought I might be trampled or beaten. We rode on the team charter coming home, eating steak and lobster. When we got to KCI, we were told the media would get off the plane first. With no cell phones, we had no idea that when the doors opened, the entire concourse would be completely full of people screaming for the team. It was surreal walking through the crowd.

3. 1988 Midwest Regional finals in Pontiac, Michigan, at the Silverdome with the unexpected KU-KSU finals for a trip to Kemper. Neither team had any business getting that far. K-State's Mitch

Richmond was awful that day. Scooter Barry did a great job frustrating him. Might have been Richmond's worst game... that I can recall.

4. Buffalo AFC title game, 1993. As close as I've been to covering a Super Bowl. Couldn't believe how all of the Bills seemed to have radio/TV shows, even Steve Tasker. The weather was brutal. Stood in the radio booth part of the game with the fans 'taunting' (fellow sportscaster) Len (Dawson) throughout the game, especially in the breaks. The out-of-town media got heckled all the way around the stadium to the visitor's locker room.

5. Super Bowl IV. I was a seventh grader at Nallwood Junior High in Overland Park at the time. I was obsessed with the Chiefs. I still have all sorts of crazy memorabilia from that era. An envelope Lenny signed for me at Metcalf South, at Christmas time. The place was packed. Lenny was going about his biz, not being bothered. My mom said, 'Honey, leave him alone.' I stopped him: 'Mr. Dawson...' And it was like piranha and bloody water. He couldn't move. I felt kinda bad, but got my autographed envelope — which I still have! I remember how 'cool' he looked. Leather bomber jacket. Gray slacks. Very cool customer.

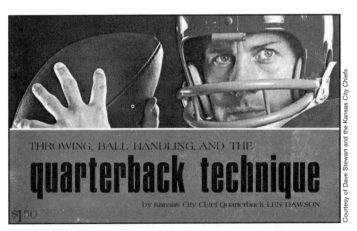

**Cover of 1969 quarterback manual featuring Len Dawson,
from Dave Stewart's personal collection**

Bibliography

Books

Allen, Marcus, with Matt Fulks, *The Road to Canton*, Champaign: Sports Publishing, 2003.

Bruce, Janet, *The Kansas City Monarchs*, Lawrence: University of Kansas Press, 1985.

Cameron, Steve, *Moments, Memories, Miracles*, Dallas: Taylor, 1992.

Corcoran, Michael, *Duel in the Sun*, New York: Simon & Schuster, 2002.

Dixon, Phil and Hannigan, Patrick, *The Negro Leagues*, Mattituck: Amereon House, 1992.

Dixon, Phil, *The Ultimate Kansas City Baseball Trivia Quiz Book*, Shawnee: Bon A Tirer, 1992.

Etkin, Jack; Nightengale, Bob; Scarbinsky, Kevin; Weinberg, Rick, *Bo Stories*, St. Louis: The Sporting News, 1990.

Feinstein, John, *Caddy for Life*, New York: Little, Brown, 2004.

Fitzgerald, Tim, *Kansas State Wildcat Handbook*, Wichita: The Wichita Eagle and Beacon, 1996.

Fox, Gene, *Sports Guys*, Lenexa: Addax: 1999.

Fulks, Matt, *CBS Sports Presents Stories from the Final Four*, Lenexa: Addax, 2000.

Fulks, Matt, *Super Bowl Sunday*, Lenexa: Addax, 2000.

Grigsby, Bill, *Grigs!*, Champaign: Sports Publishing, 2004.

Hoskins, Alan, *Warpaths*, Dallas: Taylor Publishing, 1999.

Kansas City Chiefs Media Guide, 2000.

Kansas City Comets Media Guide, 2004-05.

Kansas City Royals Media Guide, 2006.

Kansas State Basketball Media Guide, 2004-05.

Kansas State Football Media Guide, 2006.

LaBlanc, Michael L., *Professional Sports Team Histories: Basketball*, Detroit: Gale Research 1994.

Loverro, Thom, *The Encyclopedia of Negro League Baseball*, New York: Checkmark Books, 2003.

Matthews, Denny, with Matt Fulks, *Denny Matthews's Tales from the Royals Dugout*, Champaign: Sports Publishing, 2004.

Matthews, Denny, and Fred White with Matt Fulks, *Play by Play*, Lenexa: Addax, 1999.

McGuff, Joe, *Winning It All*, New York: Doubleday, 1970.

Mehl, Ernest, *The Kansas City Athletics*, New York: Henry Holt, 1956.

Metro, Charlie, *Safe by a Mile*, Lincoln: University of Nebraska Press, 2002.

Morgan, Anne, *Prescription for Success*, Kansas City: Andrews and McMeel, 1995.

O'Neil, Buck; Conrads, David; Wulf, Steve, *I Was Right on Time*, New York: Fireside, 1996.

Peterson, Brian C., *Stadium Stories: Missouri Tigers*, Guilford: Globe Pequot, 2005.

Peterson, Robert, *Only the Ball Was White*, New York: McGraw-Hill, 1984.

Stallard, Mark, *Kansas City Chiefs Encyclopedia*, Champaign: Sports Publishing, 2002.

Stallard, Mark, *Tales from the Jayhawks Gridiron*, Champaign: Sports Publishing, 2004.

Stallard, Mark, *Tales from the Jayhawks Hardwood*, Champaign: Sports Publishing, 2002.

Stram, Hank, *They're Playing My Game*, New York: William Morrow, 1986.

Taylor, Otis, with Mark Stallard, *The Need to Win*, Champaign: Sports Publishing, 2003.

The Kansas City Chapter of the Society for American Baseball Research, *Unions to Royals: The Story of Professional Baseball in Kansas City*, Jefferson: McFarland, 1996.

The Sporting News, *Baseball's 25 Greatest Moments*, St. Louis: The Sporting News, 1999.

University of Kansas Jayhawk Basketball Media Guide, 2006-07

University of Kansas Jayhawk Football Media Guide, 2006.

Weber, Stan, with David Smale, *Stan Weber's Tales from the Kansas State Sideline*, Champaign: Sports Publishing, 2005.

Newspapers

The Kansas City Star
The Kansas City Times
The Lawrence Journal-World
The Topeka Capital-Journal

Web sites

kcchiefs.com
kcmetrosports.com
mutigers.cstv.com
sportsecyclopedia.com
usopen.com

Additional Resources

Buck O'Neil's Hall of Fame speech used courtesy of the Negro Leagues Baseball Museum, Kansas City, MO.

Personal Interviews: Some of the interviews were conducted specifically for this book. Others, however, are from interviews the author had done previously for other books, newspaper or Web site articles, including those that initially ran in *The Kansas City Star*, the Royals *GameDay* magazine, and, of course, on kcmetrosports.com.

About the Author

Matt Fulks, who started his journalism career while attending Lipscomb University in Nashville, Tenn., when his baseball career was cut short by a lack of ability, spends his time as a free-lance writer, editor and broadcaster. He is a regular contributor to various publications, including kcmetrosports.com, *The Kansas City Star* newspaper and the Royals *Gameday* magazine. He is the author/co-author of ten other books, including *Echoes of Kansas Basketball, The Road to Canton,* co-authored with NFL Hall of Fame running back Marcus Allen, and *Good as Gold: Techniques for Fundamental Baseball,* with Royals legend Frank White. More information is available at www.mattfulks.com. Fulks resides in the Kansas City area with his wife Libby and their children, Helen, Charlie and Aaron.

GREGG
RIESS
Photography

WHAT'S
A PICTURE
WORTH?

GreggRiess.com

TIME WARNER CABLE
THE POWER OF YOU™

Digital Cable & HDTV
The power to watch what you want, when you want.

Road Runner
A better, faster Internet.

Digital Phone
Home phone service with unlimited long distance.

Sprint PCS®
Get ready to have more choice.

Sprint POWER UP™
Together with NEXTEL

all the best™

You'll Save Hundreds when you build a bundle that's just right for you! visit: www.saveabundle.com

GET CONNECTED!   816.358.8833

TIME WARNER CABLE
Business Class

Connect with experts who measure success by your success. Visit www.twcbizservice.com or call 816.743.2477.